The Constitution of the
State of Wyoming:
A Quick Reference Guide

Bootblack Budget Books
Copyright 2018 ©
ISBN-13: 978-1726472746
ISBN-10: 1726472744

Contents:

Preamble – Page 36

Article 1. Declaration of Rights – Page 37

Section 1. Power Inherent in the People

Section 2. Equality of All

Section 3. Equal Political Rights

Section 4. Security Against Search and Seizure

Section 5. Imprisonment for Debt

Section 6. Due Process of Law

Section 7. No Absolute, Arbitrary Power

Section 8. Courts Open to All; Suits Against State

Section 9. Trial by Jury Inviolate

Section 10. Right of Accused to Defend

Section 11. Self-Incrimination; Jeopardy

Section 12. Detaining Witnesses

Section 13. Indictment

Section 14. Bail; Cruel and Unusual Punishment

Section 15. Penal Code to be Humane

Section 16. Conduct of Jails

Section 17. Habeas Corpus

Section 18. Religious Liberty

Section 19. Appropriations for Sectarian or Religious Societies or Institutions Prohibited

Section 20. Freedom of Speech and Press; Libel; Truth a Defense

Section 21. Right of Petition and Peaceable Assembly

Section 22. Protection of Labor

Section 23. Education

Section 24. Right to Bear Arms

Section 25. Military Subordinate to Civil Power; Quartering Soldiers

Section 26. Treason

Section 27. Elections Free and Equal

Section 28. Taxation; Consent of People; Uniformity and Equality

Section 29. Rights of Aliens

Section 30. Monopolies and Perpetuities Prohibited

Section 31. Control of Water

Section 32. Eminent Domain

Section 33. Compensation for Property Taken

Section 34. Uniform Operation of General Law

Section 35. Ex Post Facto Laws; Impairing Obligation of Contracts

Section 36. Rights not Enumerated Reserved to People

Section 37. Constitution of United States Supreme Law of Land

Article 2. Distribution of Powers – Page 45

Section 1. Powers of Government Divided into Three Departments

Article 3. Legislative Department – Page 46

Section 1. Composition and Name of Legislature

Section 2. Members Terms and Qualifications

Section 3. Legislative Apportionment

Section 4. Vacancies

Section 5. When Members Elected and Terms Begin

Section 6. Compensation of Members; Duration of Sessions

Section 7. Time and Place of Sessions

Section 8. Members Disqualified for other Office

Section 9. Compensation not to be Increased During Term

Section 10. Presiding Officers; Other Officers; Each House to Judge of Election and Qualifications of it's Members

Section 11. Quorum

Section 12. Rules, Punishment and Protection

Section 13. Journals

Section 14. Sessions to be Open

Section 15. Adjournment

Section 16. Privilege of Members

Section 17. Power of Impeachment; Proceedings

Section 18. Who may be Impeached

Section 19. Removal of Officers not Subject to Impeachment

Section 20. Laws to be Passed by Bill; Alteration or Amendment of Bills

Section 21. Enacting Clause of Law

Section 22. Limitation on Time for Introducing Bill for Appropriation

Section 23. Bill Must go to Committee

Section 24. Bill to Contain Only One Subject, Which Shall be Expressed in Title

Section 25. Vote Required to Pass Bill

Section 26. How Laws Revised, Amended or Extended

Section 27. Special and Local Laws Prohibited

Section 28. Signing of Bills

Section 29. Legislative Employees

Section 30. Extra Compensation to Public Officers Prohibited

Section 31. Supplies for Legislature and Departments

Section 32. Changing Terms and Salaries of Public Officers

Section 33. Origin of Revenue Bills

Section 34. General Appropriation Bills; Other Appropriations

Section 35. Money Expended Only on Appropriation

Section 36. Prohibited Appropriations

Section 37. Delegation of Power to Perform Municipal Functions Prohibited

Section 38. Investment of Trust Funds

Section 39. Aid to Railroads Prohibited

Section 40. Debts to State or Municipal Corporation Cannot be Released Unless Otherwise Prescribed by Legislature

Section 41. Resolutions; Approval or Veto

Section 42. Bribery of Legislators and Solicitation of Bribery Defined; Expulsion of Legislator for Bribery or Solicitation

Section 43. Offers to Bribe

Section 44. Witnesses in Bribery Charges

Section 45. Legislature Shall Define Corrupt Solicitation

Section 46. Interested Member Shall not Vote

APPORTIONMENT

Section 47. Congressional Representation

Section 49. District Representation

Section 50. Apportionment for First Legislature

Section 51. Filling of Vacancies

INITIATIVE AND REFERENDUM

Section 52. Initiative and Referendum

Section 53. Creation of Criminal Penalties not Subject to Governor's Power to Commute

Article 4. Executive Department – Page 63

Section 1. Executive Power Vested in Governor; Term of Governor

Section 2. Qualifications of Governor

Section 3. Election of Governor

Section 4. Powers and Duties of Governor Generally

Section 5. Pardoning Power of Governor

Section 6. Acting Governor

Section 7. When Governor may Fill Vacancies in Office

Section 8. Approval or Veto of Legislation by Governor; Passage Over Veto

Section 9. Veto of Items of Appropriations

Section 10. Bribery or Coercion of or by Governor

Section 11. State Officers; Election; Qualifications; Terms

Section 12. State Officers; Powers and Duties

Section 13. Salaries of Governor and Other Elective State Officers

Section 14. Examination of Accounts

Article 5. Judicial Department – Page 68

Section 1. How Judicial Power Vested

Section 2. Supreme Court Generally; Appellate Jurisdiction

Section 3. Supreme Court Generally; Original Jurisdiction

Section 4. Supreme Court Generally; Number; Election of Chief Justice; Quorum; Vacancies in Supreme Court or District Court; Judicial Nominating Commission; Terms; Standing for Retention in Office

Section 5. Voluntary Retirement and Compensation of Justices and Judges

Section 6. Commission on Judicial Conduct and Ethics

Section 7. Supreme Court Generally; Terms of Court

Section 8. Supreme Court Generally; Qualifications of Justices

Section 9. Supreme Court Generally; Clerk

Section 10. District Courts Generally; Jurisdiction

Section 11. District Courts Generally; Judges to Hold Court for Each Other

Section 12. District Courts Generally; Qualifications of Judges

Section 13. District Courts Generally; Clerks

Section 14. District Courts Generally; Commissioners

Section 15. Style of Process

Section 16. Supreme Court Judges Limited to Judicial Duties

Section 17. Salaries of Judges of Supreme and District Courts

Section 18. Appeals from District Courts to Supreme Court

Section 19. State Divided Into Districts; Election and Terms of District Judges

Section 20. Districts Defined

Section 21. Increase in Number of Districts and Judges

Section 22. Jurisdiction of Justices of the Peace

Section 23. Appeals From Justices Courts

Section 24. Terms of District Courts; Attaching Unorganized Territory to Organized Counties

Section 25. Judges of Supreme and District Courts Shall Not Practice

Section 26. Power to Fix Terms of Court

Section 27. Judges of Supreme and District Courts Shall Not Hold Other Office

Section 28. Appeals from Boards of Arbitration

Section 29. Juvenile Delinquency and Domestic Relations Courts

Article 6. Suffrage and Elections – Page 81

Section 1. Male and Female Citizens to Enjoy Equal Rights

Section 2. Qualifications of Electors

Section 3. Electors Privileged From Arrest

Section 4. Exemption of Electors From Military Duty

Section 5. Electors Must be Citizens of United States

Section 6. What Persons Excluded From Franchise

Section 7. When Residence not Lost by Reason of Absence

Section 8. Soldiers Stationed in State not Considered Residents

Section 9. Educational Qualifications of Electors

Section 10. Alien Suffrage

Section 11. Manner of Holding Elections

Section 12. Registration of Voters Required

Section 13. Purity of Elections to be Provided For

Section 14. Election Contests

Section 15. Qualifications for Office

Section 16. When Officers to Hold Over; Suspension of Officers

Section 17. Time of Holding General and Special Elections; When Elected Officers to Enter Upon Duties

Section 18. Method of Selecting Officers Whose Election is not Provided For

Section 19. Dual Office Holding

Section 20. Oath of Office; Form

Section 21. Oath of Office; How Administered

Section 22. Absent Voter Ballots, Voting and Registration

Article 7. Education; State Institutions; Promotion of Health and Morals; Public Buildings – Page 87

Section 1. Legislature to Provide for Public Schools

Section 2. School Revenues

Section 3. Other Sources of School Revenues

Section 4. Restriction in Use of Revenues

Section 5. Fines and Penalties to Belong to Public School Fund

Section 6. State to Keep School Funds; Investment

Section 7. Application of School Funds

Section 8. Distribution of School Funds

Section 9. Taxation for Schools

Section 10. No Discrimination Between Pupils

Section 11. Textbooks

Section 12. Sectarianism Prohibited

Section 13. Land Commissioners

Section 14. Supervision of Schools Entrusted to State Superintendent of Public Instruction

Section 15. Establishment of University Confirmed

Section 16. Tuition Free

Section 17. Government of University

Section 18. Establishment; Supervision by State Board of Charities and Reform

Section 19. Territorial Institutions Pass to State

Section 20. Duty of Legislature to Protect and Promote Health and Morality of People

Section 21. Buildings and Property of Territory Pass to State

Section 22. Construction and Supervision

Section 23. Permanent Location

Article 8. Irrigation and Water Rights – Page 94

Section 1. Water is State Property

Section 2. Board of Control

Section 3. Priority of Appropriation

Section 4. Water Divisions

Section 5. State Engineer

Article 9. Mines and Mining – Page 95

Section 1. Inspector of Mines

Section 2. Legislature to Enact Regulatory Laws

Section 3. Restrictions on Employment in Mines

Section 4. Right of Action for Injuries

Section 5. School of Mines

Section 6. State Geologist

Article 10. Corporations – Page 96

Section 1. Creation

Section 2. Control by State

Section 3. Forfeited Charters

Section 4. Damages for Personal Injuries or Death; Worker's Compensation

Section 5. Acceptance of Constitution

Section 6. Engaging in More Than One Line of Business

Section 7. What Corporations are Common Carriers

Section 8. Trusts Prohibited

Section 9. Eminent Domain

Section 10. Mutual and Co-Operative associations

Section 11. Powers and Rights of Railroads

Section 12. Discrimination by Railroads and Telegraph Lines Forbidden

Section 13. Railroads to Make Annual Reports to State Auditor

Section 14. Eminent Domain

Section 15. Aid to Railroads and Telegraph Lines Prohibited

Section 16. Acceptance of Constitution by Existing Railroad, Transportation and Telegraph Companies

Section 17. Rights of Telegraph Companies

Section 18. Foreign Railroad or Telegraph Company Must Have Agent for Service of Process

Section 19. Location of Depots

Article 11. Boundaries – Page 101

Section 1. State Boundaries

Article 12. County Organization – Page 102

Section 1. Existing Counties Remain Such

Section 2. Organization of New Counties

Section 3. Changing County Seats

Section 4. Township Organization

Section 5. County Officers

Article 13. Municipal Corporations – Page 104

Section 1. Incorporation; Alteration of Boundaries; Merger; Consolidation; Dissolution; Determination of Local Affairs; Classification; Referendum; Liberal Construction

Section 2. Consent of Electors Necessary

Section 3. Restriction on Powers to Levy Taxes and Contract Debts

Section 4. Franchises

Section 5. Acquisition of Water Rights

Article 14. Public Officers – Page 108

Section 1. Stated Salaries to be Paid

Section 2. Fees

Section 3. Legislature to Designate County Offices and Fix Salaries of County Officers

Section 4. Deputies

Section 5. Who are County Officers Referred to by Section 3

Section 6. Consolidation of Offices

Article 15. Taxation and Revenue – Page 110

Section 1. Assessment of Lands and Improvements Thereon

Section 2. Assessment of Coal Lands

Section 3. Taxation of Mines and Mining Claims

Section 4. State Levy Limited

Section 5. County Levies Limited

Section 6. City Levies Limited

Section 7. Depositories for Public Moneys

Section 8. Profit Making From Public Funds Prohibited

Section 9. Legislature to Provide for State Board of Equalization

Section 10. Duties of State Board of Equalization

Section 11. Uniformity of Assessment Required

Section 12. Exemptions From Taxation

Section 13. Tax Must be Authorized by Law; Law to State Object

Section 14. Surrender of Taxing Power Prohibited

Section 15. State Tax for Support of Public Schools

Section 16. Disposition of Fees, Excises and License Taxes on Vehicles and Gasoline

Section 17. County Levy for Support and Maintenance of Public Schools

Section 18. Full Tax Credit Allowed Against any Liability Arising From a Tax on Income

Section 19. Mineral Excise Tax; Distribution

Section 20. Higher Education Trust Funds; Investments; Earnings

Article 16. Public Indebtedness – Page 116

Section 1. Limitation on State Debt

Section 2. Creation of State Debt in Excess of Taxes for Current Year

Section 3. Limitation on County Debt

Section 4. Creation of County or Municipal Debt in Excess of Taxes for Current Year

Section 5. Limitation on Municipal, County or School District Debt

Section 6. Loan of Credit; Donations Prohibited; Works of Internal Improvement

Section 7. Payments of Public Money

Section 8. Endorsements Required on Bonds and Other Evidences of Indebtedness

Section 9. Construction and Improvement of Public Roads and Highways

Section 10. Construction and Improvement of Works for Conservation and Utilization of Water

Section 11. Construction, Maintenance and Improvement of Public Airports, Aircraft Landing Strips and Related Facilities

Section 12. Economic Development Loan Fund

Section 13. Industrial and Economic Development; Powers of Counties and Municipalities

Article 17. State Militia – Page 122

Section 1. Of Whom Militia Constituted

Section 2. Legislature to Provide for Enrollment, Equipment and Discipline

Section 3. How Officers Commissioned

Section 4. Flags

Section 5. Governor to be Commander-in-Chief; Powers

Article 18. Public Lands and Donations – Page 124

Section 1. Acceptance of Lands From United States; Sale of Such Lands

Section 2. Application of Proceeds of Sale or Rental

Section 3. Board of Land Commissioners

Section 4. Legislature to Provide for Disposition of Lands

Section 5. Special Privileges Prohibited

Section 6. Disposition of Unexpended Income of Perpetual School Fund

Article 19. Miscellaneous – Page 127

Livestock

Section 1. Legislature to Provide for Protection of Livestock and Stock Owners

Labor

Section 2. Day's Work

Labor on Public Works

Section 3. Who shall not be employed on public works.

Section 4. Legislature to Provide for Enforcement of Section 3

Boards of Arbitration

Section 5. Legislature to Establish Courts of Arbitration; Duties

Police Powers

Section 6. Importing Armed Bodies to Suppress Violence Prohibited; Exception

Labor Contracts

Section 7. Contract Exempting Employer from Liability for Personal Injuries Prohibited

Arbitration

Section 8. Legislature to Provide for Voluntary Submission of Differences to Arbitrators

Homesteads

Section 9. Exemption of Homestead

Intoxicating Liquors

Section 10. Intoxicating Liquors

Section 11. Use of Monies in Public Employee Retirement Funds Restricted

Article 20. Amendments – Page 131

Section 1. How Amendments Proposed by Legislature and Submitted to People

Section 2. How Two or More Amendments Voted On

Section 3. Constitutional Convention

Section 4. Constitution Adopted by Convention to be Submitted to People

Article 21. Schedule – Page 133

Section 1. Acquired Rights Continue

Section 2. Territorial Property Vested in State

Section 3. Territorial Laws Become State Laws

Section 4. Accrued Fines go to State

Section 5. State to Sue on Bonds and Prosecute Crimes

Section 6. Territorial Officers to Hold Over

Section 7. Submission of Constitution

Section 8. When Constitution Takes Effect

Section 9. First State Election; Time of Holding; Proclamation

Section 10. First State Election; Duty of County Commissioners; Who May Vote; Conduct of Election

Section 11. First State Election; Board of Canvassers

Section 12. When Officers Shall Qualify; Oaths; Bonds

Section 13. First State Legislature

Section 14. Laws to be Passed

Section 15. Transfer of Pending Causes, Records and Seal of Courts

Section 16. Court Seals

Section 17. Transfer of Causes and Records From Probate Courts to District Courts

Section 18. How Legislature Chosen

Section 19. Duration of Terms of Territorial County and Precinct Officers

Section 20. Terms of State Officers First Elected

Section 21. Regular Session of Legislature Following First Session

Section 22. Regular Election Following First Session of Legislature to be Omitted

Section 23. Why Constitution Framed

Ordinances – Page 141

Section 24. State Part of United States

Section 25. Religious Liberty

Section 26. Ownership of Certain Lands Disclaimed; Restriction on Taxation of Nonresidents

Section 27. Territorial Liabilities Assumed

Section 28. Legislature to Provide for Public Schools

PREAMBLE

We, the people of the State of Wyoming, grateful to God for our civil, political and religious liberties, and desiring to secure them to ourselves and perpetuate them to our posterity, do ordain and establish this Constitution.

ARTICLE 1. DECLARATION OF RIGHTS

Section 1. Power Inherent in the People

All power is inherent in the people, and all free governments are founded on their authority, and instituted for their peace, safety and happiness; for the advancement of these ends they have at all times an inalienable and indefeasible right to alter, reform or abolish the government in such manner as they may think proper.

Section 2. Equality of All

In their inherent right to life, liberty and the pursuit of happiness, all members of the human race are equal.

Section 3. Equal Political Rights

Since equality in the enjoyment of natural and civil rights is only made sure through political equality, the laws of this state affecting the political rights and privileges of its citizens shall be without distinction of race, color, sex, or any circumstance or condition whatsoever other than individual incompetency, or unworthiness duly ascertained by a court of competent jurisdiction.

Section 4. Security Against Search and Seizure

The right of the people to be secure in their persons, houses, papers and effects against unreasonable searches and seizures shall not be violated, and no warrant shall issue but upon probable cause, supported by affidavit, particularly describing the place to be searched or the person or thing to be seized.

Section 5. Imprisonment for Debt

No person shall be imprisoned for debt, except in cases of fraud.

Section 6. Due Process of Law

No person shall be deprived of life, liberty or property without due process of law.

Section 7. No Absolute, Arbitrary Power

Absolute, arbitrary power over the lives, liberty and property of freemen exists nowhere in a republic, not even in the largest majority.

Section 8. Courts Open to All; Suits Against State

All courts shall be open and every person for an injury done to person, reputation or property shall have justice administered without sale, denial or delay. Suits may be brought against the state in such manner and in such courts as the legislature may by law direct.

Section 9. Trial by Jury Inviolate

The right of trial by jury shall remain inviolate in criminal cases. A jury in civil cases and in criminal cases where the charge is a misdemeanor may consist of less than twelve (12) persons but not less than six (6), as may be prescribed by law. A grand jury may consist of twelve (12) persons, any nine (9) of whom concurring may find an indictment. The legislature may change, regulate or abolish the grand jury system.

Section 10. Right of Accused to Defend

In all criminal prosecutions the accused shall have the right to defend in person and by counsel, to demand the nature and cause of the accusation, to have a copy thereof, to be confronted with the witnesses against him, to have compulsory process served for obtaining witnesses, and to a speedy trial by an impartial jury of the county or district in which the offense is alleged to have been committed. When the location of the offense cannot be established with certainty, venue may be placed in the county or district where the corpus delecti [delicti] is found, or in any county or district in which the victim was transported.

Section 11. Self-Incrimination; Jeopardy

No person shall be compelled to testify against himself in any criminal case, nor shall any person be twice put in jeopardy for the same offense. If a jury disagree, or if the judgment be arrested after a verdict, or if the judgment be reversed for error in law, the accused shall not be deemed to have been in jeopardy.

Section 12. Detaining Witnesses

No person shall be detained as a witness in any criminal prosecution longer than may be necessary to take his testimony or deposition, nor be confined in any room where criminals are imprisoned.

Section 13. Indictment

Until otherwise provided by law, no person shall, for a felony, be proceeded against criminally, otherwise than by indictment, except in cases arising in the land or naval forces, or in the militia when in actual service in time of war or public danger.

Section 14. Bail; Cruel and Unusual Punishment

All persons shall be bailable by sufficient sureties, except for capital offenses when the proof is evident or the presumption great. Excessive bail shall not be required, nor excessive fines imposed, nor shall cruel or unusual punishment be inflicted.

Section 15. Penal Code to be Humane

The penal code shall be framed on the humane principles of reformation and prevention.

Section 16. Conduct of Jails

No person arrested and confined in jail shall be treated with unnecessary rigor. The erection of safe and comfortable prisons, and inspection of prisons, and the humane treatment of prisoners shall be provided for.

Section 17. Habeas Corpus

The privilege of the writ of habeas corpus shall not be suspended unless, when in case of rebellion or invasion the public safety may require it.

Section 18. Religious Liberty

The free exercise and enjoyment of religious profession and worship without discrimination or preference shall be forever guaranteed in this state, and no person shall be rendered incompetent to hold any office of trust or profit, or to serve as a witness or juror, because of his opinion on any matter of religious belief whatever; but the liberty of conscience hereby secured shall not be so construed as to excuse acts of licentiousness or justify practices inconsistent with the peace or safety of the state.

Section 19. Appropriations for Sectarian or Religious Societies or Institutions Prohibited

No money of the state shall ever be given or appropriated to any sectarian or religious society or institution.

Section 20. Freedom of Speech and Press; Libel; Truth a Defense

Every person may freely speak, write and publish on all subjects, being responsible for the abuse of that right; and in all trials for libel, both civil and criminal, the truth, when published with good intent and [for] justifiable ends, shall be a sufficient defense, the jury having the right to determine the facts and the law, under direction of the court.

Section 21. Right of Petition and Peaceable Assembly

The right of petition, and of the people peaceably to assemble to consult for the common good, and to make known their opinions, shall never be denied or abridged.

Section 22. Protection of Labor

The rights of labor shall have just protection through laws calculated to secure to the laborer proper rewards for his service and to promote the industrial welfare of the state.

Section 23. Education

The right of the citizens to opportunities for education should have practical recognition. The legislature shall suitably encourage means and agencies calculated to advance the sciences and liberal arts.

Section 24. Right to Bear Arms

The right of citizens to bear arms in defense of themselves and of the state shall not be denied.

Section 25. Military Subordinate to Civil Power; Quartering Soldiers

The military shall ever be in strict subordination to the civil power. No soldier in time of peace shall be quartered in any house without consent of the owner, nor in time of war except in the manner prescribed by law.

Section 26. Treason

Treason against the state shall consist only in levying war against it, or in adhering to its enemies, or in giving them aid and comfort. No person shall be convicted of treason unless on the testimony of two witnesses to the same overt act, or on confession in open court; nor shall any person be attained of treason by the legislature.

Section 27. Elections Free and Equal

Elections shall be open, free and equal, and no power, civil or military, shall at any time interfere to prevent an untrammeled exercise of the right of suffrage.

Section 28. Taxation; Consent of People; Uniformity and Equality

No tax shall be imposed without the consent of the people or their authorized representatives.

Section 29. Rights of Aliens

No distinction shall ever be made by law between resident aliens and citizens as to the possession, taxation, enjoyment and descent of property.

Section 30. Monopolies and Perpetuities Prohibited

Perpetuities and monopolies are contrary to the genius of a free state, and shall not be allowed. Corporations being creatures of the state, endowed for the public good with a portion of its sovereign powers, must be subject to its control.

Section 31. Control of Water

Water being essential to industrial prosperity, of limited amount, and easy of diversion from its natural channels, its control must be in the state, which, in providing for its use, shall equally guard all the various interests involved.

Section 32. Eminent Domain

Private property shall not be taken for private use unless by consent of the owner, except for private ways of necessity, and for reservoirs, drains, flumes or ditches on or across the lands of others for agricultural, mining, milling, domestic or sanitary purposes, nor in any case without due compensation.

Section 33. Compensation for Property Taken

Private property shall not be taken or damaged for public or private use without just compensation.

Section 34. Uniform Operation of General Law

All laws of a general nature shall have a uniform operation.

Section 35. Ex Post Facto Laws; Impairing Obligation of Contracts

No ex post facto law, nor any law impairing the obligation of contracts, shall ever be made.

Section 36. Rights not Enumerated Reserved to People

The enumeration in this constitution, of certain rights shall not be construed to deny, impair, or disparage others retained by the people.

Section 37. Constitution of United States Supreme Law of Land

The State of Wyoming is an inseparable part of the federal union, and the constitution of the United States is the supreme law of the land.

ARTICLE 2. DISTRIBUTION OF POWERS

Section 1. Powers of Government Divided into Three Departments

The powers of the government of this state are divided into three distinct departments: The legislative, executive and judicial, and no person or collection of persons charged with the exercise of powers properly belonging to one of these departments shall exercise any powers properly belonging to either of the others, except as in this constitution expressly directed or permitted.

ARTICLE 3. LEGISLATIVE DEPARTMENT

Section 1. Composition and Name of Legislature

The legislative power shall be vested in a senate and house of representatives, which shall be designated "the legislature of the State of Wyoming."

Section 2. Members Terms and Qualifications

Senators shall be elected for the term of four (4) years and representatives for the term of two (2) years. The senators elected at the first election shall be divided by lot into two classes as nearly equal as may be. The seats of senators of the first class shall be vacated at the expiration of the first two years, and of the second class at the expiration of four years. No person shall be a senator who has not attained the age of twenty-five years, or a representative who has not attained the age of twenty-one years, and who is not a citizen of the United States and of this state and who has not, for at least twelve months next preceding his election resided within the county or district in which he was elected.

Section 3. Legislative Apportionment

Each county shall constitute a senatorial and representative district; the senate and house of representatives shall be composed of members elected by the legal voters of the counties respectively, every two (2) years. They shall be apportioned among the said counties as nearly as may be according to the number of their inhabitants. Each county shall have at least one senator and one representative; but at no time shall the number of members of the house of representatives be less than twice nor greater than three times the number of members of the senate. The senate and house of representatives first elected in pursuance of this constitution shall consist of sixteen and thirty-three members respectively.

Section 4. Vacancies

Repealed

Section 5. When Members Elected and Terms Begin

Members of the senate and house of representatives shall be elected on the day provided by law for the general election of a member of congress, and their term of office shall begin on the first Monday of January thereafter.

Section 6. Compensation of Members; Duration of Sessions

The legislature shall not meet for more than sixty (60) legislative working days excluding Sundays during the term for which members of the house of representatives are elected, except when called into special session. The legislature shall determine by statute the number of days not to exceed sixty (60) legislative working days to be devoted to general and budget session, respectively. The legislature shall meet on odd-numbered years for a general and budget session. The legislature may meet on even-numbered years for budget session. During the budget session no bills except the budget bill may be introduced unless placed on call by a two-thirds vote of either house. The legislature shall meet for no more than forty (40) legislative working days excluding Sundays in any one (1) calendar year, except when called into special session. The compensation of the members of the legislature shall be as provided by law; but no legislature shall fix its own compensation.

Section 7. Time and Place of Sessions

The legislature shall meet at the seat of government at twelve o'clock noon, on the second Tuesday of January of the odd-numbered years for general and budget session and may meet on the second Tuesday of January of the even-numbered years for budget session, and at other times when convened by the governor or upon call of the legislature as herein provided. The governor by proclamation may also, in times of war or grave emergency by law defined, temporarily convene the legislature at a place or places other than the seat of government. The legislature may convene a special session not to last longer than twenty (20) working days as follows:

(i) Upon written request to the presiding officer of each house of the legislature by a majority of the elected members of each house, the legislature shall convene in a special session; or

(ii) The presiding officers of each house shall also jointly call a special session for the purpose of resolving a challenge or a dispute of any kind in the determination of the presidential electors.

Section 8. Members Disqualified for other Office

No senator or representative shall, during the term for which he was elected, be appointed to any civil office under the state, and no member of congress or other person holding an office (except that of notary public or an office in the militia) under the United States or this state, shall be a member of either house during his continuance in office.

Section 9. Compensation not to be Increased During Term

No member of either house shall, during the term for which he was elected, receive any increase of salary or mileage under any law passed during that term.

Section 10. Presiding Officers; Other Officers; Each House to Judge of Election and Qualifications of it's Members

The senate shall, at the beginning and close of each regular session and at such other times as may be necessary, elect one of its members president; the house of representatives shall elect one of its members speaker; each house shall choose its other officers, and shall judge of the election returns and qualifications of its members.

Section 11. Quorum

A majority of each house shall constitute a quorum to do business, but a smaller number may adjourn from day to day, and compel the attendance of absent members in such manner and under such penalties as each house may prescribe.

Section 12. Rules, Punishment and Protection

Each house shall have power to determine the rules of its proceedings, and [to] punish its members or other persons for contempt or disorderly behavior in its presence; to protect its members against violence or offers of bribes or private solicitation, and with the concurrence of two-thirds, to expel a member, and shall have all other powers necessary to the legislature of a free state. A member expelled for corruption shall not thereafter be eligible to either house of the legislature, and punishment for contempt or disorderly behavior shall not bar a criminal prosecution for the same offense.

Section 13. Journals

Each house shall keep a journal of its proceedings and may, in its discretion, from time to time, publish the same, except such parts as require secrecy, and the yeas and nays on any question, shall, at the request of any two members, be entered on the journal.

Section 14. Sessions to be Open

The sessions of each house and of the committee of the whole shall be open unless the business is such as requires secrecy.

Section 15. Adjournment

Neither house shall, without the consent of the other, adjourn for more than three days, nor to any other place than that in which the two houses shall be sitting.

Section 16. Privilege of Members

The members of the legislature shall, in all cases, except treason, felony, violation of their oath of office and breach of the peace, be privileged from arrest during their attendance at the sessions of their respective houses, and in going to and returning from the same; and for any speech or debate in either house they shall not be questioned in any other place.

Section 17. Power of Impeachment; Proceedings

The sole power of impeachment shall vest in the house of representatives; the concurrence of a majority of all the members being necessary to the exercise thereof. Impeachment shall be tried by the senate sitting for that purpose, and the senators shall be upon oath or affirmation to do justice according to law and evidence. When the governor is on trial, the chief justice of the supreme court shall preside. No person shall be convicted without a concurrence of two-thirds of the senators elected.

Section 18. Who may be Impeached

The governor and other state and judicial officers except justices of the peace, shall be liable to impeachment for high crimes and misdemeanors, or malfeasance in office, but judgment in such cases shall only extend to removal from office and disqualification to hold any office of honor, trust or profit under the laws of the state. The party, whether convicted or acquitted, shall, nevertheless, be liable to prosecution, trial, judgment and punishment according to law.

Section 19. Removal of Officers not Subject to Impeachment

Except as hereafter provided, all officers not liable to impeachment shall be subject to removal for misconduct or malfeasance in office as provided by law. Any person appointed by the governor to serve as head of a state agency, or division thereof, or to serve as a member of a state board or commission, may be removed by the governor as provided by law.

Section 20. Laws to be Passed by Bill; Alteration or Amendment of Bills

No law shall be passed except by bill, and no bill shall be so altered or amended on its passage through either house as to change its original purpose.

Section 21. Enacting Clause of Law

The enacting clause of every law shall be as follows: "Be it Enacted by the Legislature of the State of Wyoming."

Section 22. Limitation on Time for Introducing Bill for Appropriation

No bill for the appropriation of money, except for the expenses of the government, shall be introduced within five (5) days of the close of the session, except by unanimous consent of the house in which it is sought to be introduced.

Section 23. Bill Must go to Committee

No bill shall be considered or become a law unless referred to a committee, returned therefrom and printed for the use of the members.

Section 24. Bill to Contain Only One Subject, Which Shall be Expressed in Title

No bill, except general appropriation bills and bills for the codification and general revision of the laws, shall be passed containing more than one subject, which shall be clearly expressed in its title; but if any subject is embraced in any act which is not expressed in the title, such act shall be void only as to so much thereof as shall not be so expressed.

Section 25. Vote Required to Pass Bill

No bill shall become a law except by a vote of a majority of all the members elected to each house, nor unless on its final passage the vote taken by ayes and noes, and the names of those voting be entered on the journal.

Section 26. How Laws Revised, Amended or Extended

No law shall be revised or amended, or the provisions thereof extended by reference to its title only, but so much thereof as is revised, amended, or extended, shall be re-enacted and published at length.

Section 27. Special and Local Laws Prohibited

The legislature shall not pass local or special laws in any of the following enumerated cases, that is to say: For granting divorces; laying out, opening, altering or working roads or highways; vacating roads, town plats, streets, alleys or public grounds; locating or changing county seats; regulating county or township affairs; incorporation of cities, towns or villages; or changing or amending the charters of any cities, towns or villages; regulating the practice in courts of justice; regulating the jurisdiction and duties of justices of the peace, police magistrates or constables; changing the rules of evidence in any trial or inquiry; providing for changes of venue in civil or criminal cases; declaring any person of age; for limitation of civil actions; giving effect to any informal or invalid deeds; summoning or impaneling grand or petit juries; providing for the management of common schools; regulating the rate of interest on money; the opening or conducting of any election or designating the place of voting; the sale or mortgage of real estate belonging to minors or others under disability; chartering or licensing ferries or bridges or toll roads; chartering banks, insurance companies and loan and trust companies; remitting fines, penalties or forfeitures; creating, increasing, or decreasing fees, percentages or allowances of public officers; changing the law of descent; granting to any corporation, association or individual, the right to lay down railroad tracks, or any special or exclusive privilege, immunity or franchise whatever, or amending existing charter for such purpose; for punishment of crimes; changing the names of persons or places; for the assessment or collection of taxes; affecting estates of deceased persons, minors or others under legal disabilities; extending the time for the collection of taxes; refunding money paid into the state treasury, relinquishing or extinguishing, in whole or part, the indebtedness, liabilities or obligation of any corporation or person to this state or to any municipal corporation therein; exempting property from taxation; restoring to citizenship persons convicted of infamous crimes; authorizing the creation, extension or impairing of liens; creating offices or prescribing the powers or duties of officers in counties, cities, townships or school districts; or authorizing the adoption or legitimation of children. In all other cases where a general law can be made applicable no special law shall be enacted.

Section 28. Signing of Bills

The presiding officer of each house shall, in the presence of the house over which he presides, sign all bills and joint resolutions passed by the legislature immediately after their titles have been publicly read, and the fact of signing shall be at once entered upon the journal.

Section 29. Legislative Employees

The legislature shall prescribe by law the number, duties and compensation of the officers and employes of each house, and no payment shall be made from the state treasury, or be in any way authorized to any such person except to an acting officer or employee elected or appointed in pursuance of law.

Section 30. Extra Compensation to Public Officers Prohibited

No bill shall be passed giving any extra compensation to any public officer, servant or employee, agent or contractor, after services are rendered or contract made.

Section 31. Supplies for Legislature and Departments

All stationery, printing, paper, fuel and lights used in the legislature and other departments of government shall be furnished, and the printing and binding of the laws, journals and department reports and other printing and binding, and the repairing and furnishing the halls and rooms used for the meeting of the legislature and its committees shall be performed under contract, to be given to the lowest responsible bidder, below such maximum price and under such regulations as may be prescribed by law. No member or officer of any department of the government shall be in any way interested in any such contract; and all such contracts shall be subject to the approval of the governor and state treasurer.

Section 32. Changing Terms and Salaries of Public Officers

Except as otherwise provided in this constitution, no law shall extend the term of any public officer or increase or diminish his salary or emolument after his election or appointment; but this shall not be construed to forbid the legislature from fixing salaries or emoluments of those officers first elected or appointed under this constitution, if such salaries or emoluments are not fixed by its provisions.

Section 33. Origin of Revenue Bills

All bills for raising revenue shall originate in the house of representatives; but the senate may propose amendments, as in case of other bills.

Section 34. General Appropriation Bills; Other Appropriations

The general appropriation bills shall embrace nothing but appropriations for the ordinary expenses of the legislative, executive and judicial departments of the state, interest on the public debt, and for public schools. All other appropriations shall be made by separate bills, each embracing but one subject.

Section 35. Money Expended Only on Appropriation

Except for interest on public debt, money shall be paid out of the treasury only on appropriations made by the legislature, and in no case otherwise than upon warrant drawn by the proper officer in pursuance of law.

Section 36. Prohibited Appropriations

No appropriation shall be made for charitable, industrial, educational or benevolent purposes to any person, corporation or community not under the absolute control of the state, nor to any denominational or sectarian institution or association.

Section 37. Delegation of Power to Perform Municipal Functions Prohibited

The legislature shall not delegate to any special commissioner, private corporation or association, any power to make, supervise or interfere with any municipal improvements, moneys, property or effects, whether held in trust or otherwise, to levy taxes, or to perform any municipal functions whatever.

Section 38. Investment of Trust Funds

The legislature may authorize the investment of trust funds by executors, administrators, guardians or trustees, in the bonds or stocks of private corporations, and in such other securities as it may by law provide.

Section 39. Aid to Railroads Prohibited

The legislature shall have no power to pass any law authorizing the state or any county in the state to contract any debt or obligation in the construction of any railroad, or give or loan its credit to or in aid of the construction of the same.

Section 40. Debts to State or Municipal Corporation Cannot be Released Unless Otherwise Prescribed by Legislature

No obligation or liability of any person, association or corporation held or owned by the state or any municipal corporation therein shall ever be exchanged, transferred, remitted, released, postponed or in any way diminished except as may be prescribed by the legislature. The liability or obligation shall not be extinguished except by payment into the proper treasury or as may otherwise be prescribed by the legislature in cases where the obligation or liability is not collectible.

Section 41. Resolutions; Approval or Veto

Every order, resolution or vote, in which the concurrence of both houses may be necessary, except on the question of adjournment, or relating solely to the transaction of the business of the two houses, shall be presented to the governor, and before it shall take effect be approved by him, or, being disapproved, be repassed by two-thirds of both houses as prescribed in the case of a bill.

Section 42. Bribery of Legislators and Solicitation of Bribery Defined; Expulsion of Legislator for Bribery or Solicitation

If any person elected to either house of the legislature shall offer or promise to give his vote or influence in favor of or against any measure or proposition, pending or to be introduced into the legislature, in consideration or upon condition that any other person elected to the same legislature will give, or promise or assent to give his vote or influence in favor of or against any other measure or proposition pending or proposed to be introduced into such legislature, the person making such offer or promise shall be deemed guilty of solicitation of bribery. If any member of the legislature shall give his vote or influence for or against any measure or proposition pending or to be introduced in such legislature, or offer, promise or assent thereto, upon condition that any other member will give or will promise or assent to give his vote or influence in favor of or against any other measure or proposition pending or to be introduced in such legislature, or in consideration that any other member has given his vote or influence for or against any other measure or proposition in such legislature, he shall be deemed guilty of bribery, and any member of the legislature, or person elected thereto, who shall be guilty of either of such offenses, shall be expelled and shall not thereafter be eligible to the legislature, and on conviction thereof in the civil courts shall be liable to such further penalty as may be prescribed by law.

Section 43. Offers to Bribe

Any person who shall directly or indirectly offer, give or promise any money or thing of value, testimonial, privilege or personal advantage, to any executive or judicial officer or member of the legislature, to influence him in the performance of any of his official duties shall be deemed guilty of bribery, and be punished in such manner as shall be provided by law.

Section 44. Witnesses in Bribery Charges

Any person may be compelled to testify in any lawful investigation or judicial proceeding against any person who may be charged with having committed the offense of bribery or corrupt solicitation, or practices of solicitation, and shall not be permitted to withhold his testimony upon the ground that it may criminate himself, or subject him to public infamy; but such testimony shall not afterwards be used against him in any judicial proceeding, except for perjury in giving such testimony, and any person convicted of either of the offenses aforesaid shall, as part of the punishment therefor, be disqualified from holding any office or position of honor, trust or profit in this state.

Section 45. Legislature Shall Define Corrupt Solicitation

The offense of corrupt solicitation of members of the legislature or of public officers of the state, or of any municipal division thereof, and the occupation or practice of solicitation of such members or officers to influence their official actions shall be defined by law and shall be punishable by fine and imprisonment.

Section 46. Interested Member Shall not Vote

A member who has a personal or private interest in any measure or bill proposed or pending before the legislature shall disclose the fact to the house of which he is a member, and shall not vote thereon.

APPORTIONMENT

Section 47. Congressional Representation

One representative in the congress of the United States shall be elected from the state at large, the Tuesday next after the first Monday in November, 1890, and thereafter at such times and places, and in such manner as may be prescribed by law. When a

new apportionment shall be made by congress, the legislature shall divide the state into congressional districts accordingly.
Section 48. State census. At the first budget session of the legislature following the federal census, the legislature shall reapportion its membership based upon that census. Notwithstanding any other provision of this article, any bill to apportion the legislature may be introduced in a budget session in the same manner as in a general session.

Section 49. District Representation

Congressional districts may be altered from time to time as public convenience may require. When a congressional district shall be composed of two or more counties they shall be contiguous, and the districts as compact as may be. No county shall be divided in the formation of congressional districts.

Section 50. Apportionment for First Legislature

Until an apportionment of senators and representatives as otherwise provided by law, they shall be divided among the several counties of the state in the following manner: Albany County, two senators and five representatives. Carbon County, two senators and five representatives. Converse County, one senator and three representatives. Crook County, one senator and two representatives. Fremont County, one senator and two representatives. Laramie County, three senators and six representatives. Johnson County, one senator and two representatives. Sheridan County, one senator and two representatives. Sweetwater County, two senators and three representatives. Uinta County, two senators and three representatives.

Section 51. Filling of Vacancies

When vacancies shall occur in the membership of either house of the legislature of the State of Wyoming through death, resignation or other cause, such vacancies shall be filled in such manner as may be prescribed by law, notwithstanding the provisions of section 4 of article III of the constitution which is by this section repealed.

INITIATIVE AND REFERENDUM

Section 52. Initiative and Referendum

(a) The people may propose and enact laws by the initiative, and approve or reject acts of the legislature by the referendum.

(b) An initiative or referendum is proposed by an application containing the bill to be initiated or the act to be referred. The application shall be signed by not less than one hundred (100) qualified voters as sponsors, and shall be filed with the secretary of state. If he finds it in proper form he shall so certify. Denial of certification shall be subject to judicial review.

(c) After certification of the application, a petition containing a summary of the subject matter shall be prepared by the secretary of state for circulation by the sponsors. The petition may be filed with the secretary of state if it meets both of the following requirements:

(i) It is signed by qualified voters, equal in number to fifteen percent (15%) of those who voted in the preceding general election; and

(ii) It is signed by qualified voters equal in number to fifteen percent (15%) of those resident in at least two-thirds (2/3) of the counties of the state, as determined by those who voted in the preceding general election in that county.

(d) An initiative petition may be filed at any time except that one may not be filed for a measure substantially the same as that defeated by an initiative election within the preceding five (5) years. The secretary of state shall prepare a ballot title and proposition summarizing the proposed law, and shall place them on the ballot for the first statewide election held more than one hundred twenty (120) days after adjournment of the legislative session following the filing. If, before the election, substantially the same measure has been enacted, the petition is void.

(e) A referendum petition may be filed only within ninety (90) days after adjournment of the legislative session at which the act was passed, except that a referendum petition respecting any act previously passed by the legislature may be filed within six months after the power of referendum is adopted. The secretary of state shall prepare a ballot title and proposition summarizing the act and shall place them on the ballot for the first statewide election held more than one hundred eighty (180) days after adjournment of that session.

(f) If votes in an amount in excess of fifty percent (50%) of those voting in the general election are cast in favor of adoption of an initiated measure, the measure is enacted. If votes in an amount in excess of fifty percent (50%) of those voted in the general election are cast in favor of rejection of an act referred, it is rejected. The secretary of state shall certify the election returns. An initiated law becomes effective ninety (90) days after certification, is not subject to veto, and may not be repealed by the legislature within two (2) years of its effective date. It may be amended at any time. An act rejected by referendum is void thirty (30) days after certification. Additional procedures for the initiative and referendum may be prescribed by law.

(g) The initiative shall not be used to dedicate revenues, make or repeal appropriations, create courts, define the jurisdiction of courts or prescribe their rules, enact local or special legislation, or enact that prohibited by the constitution for enactment by the legislature. The referendum shall not be applied to dedications of revenue, to appropriations, to local or special legislation, or to laws necessary for the immediate preservation of the public peace, health or safety.

Section 53. Creation of Criminal Penalties not Subject to Governor's Power to Commute

Notwithstanding Article 4, Section 5 of this Constitution, the legislature may by law create a penalty of life imprisonment without parole for specified crimes which sentence shall not be subject to commutation by the governor. The legislature may in addition limit commutation of a death sentence to a sentence of life imprisonment without parole which sentence shall not be subject to further commutation. In no event shall the inherent power of the governor to grant a pardon be limited or curtailed.

ARTICLE 4. EXECUTIVE DEPARTMENT

Section 1. Executive Power Vested in Governor; Term of Governor

The executive power shall be vested in a governor, who shall hold his office for the term of four (4) years and until his successor is elected and duly qualified.

Section 2. Qualifications of Governor

No person shall be eligible to the office of governor unless he be a citizen of the United States and a qualified elector of the state, who has attained the age of thirty years, and who has resided 5 years next preceding the election within the state or territory, nor shall he be eligible to any other office during the term for which he was elected.

Section 3. Election of Governor

The governor shall be elected by the qualified electors of the state at the time and place of choosing members of the legislature. The person having the highest number of votes for governor shall be declared elected, but if two or more shall have an equal and highest number of votes for governor, the two houses of the legislature at its next regular session shall forthwith, by joint ballot, choose one of such persons for said office. The returns of the election for governor shall be made in such manner as shall be prescribed by law.

Section 4. Powers and Duties of Governor Generally

The governor shall be commander-in-chief of the military forces of the state, except when they are called into the service of the United States, and may call out the same to execute the laws, suppress insurrection and repel invasion. He shall have power to convene the legislature on extraordinary occasions. He shall at the commencement of each session communicate to the legislature by message, information of the condition of the state, and recommend such measures as he shall deem expedient. He shall transact all necessary business with the officers of the government, civil and military. He shall expedite all such measures as may be resolved upon by the legislature and shall take care that the laws be faithfully executed.

Section 5. Pardoning Power of Governor

The governor shall have power to remit fines and forfeitures, to grant reprieves, commutations and pardons after conviction, for all offenses except treason and cases of impeachment; but the legislature may by law regulate the manner in which the remission of fines, pardons, commutations and reprieves may be applied for. Upon conviction for treason he shall have power to suspend the execution of sentence until the case is reported to the legislature at its next regular session, when the legislature shall either pardon, or commute the sentence, direct the execution of the sentence or grant further reprieve. He shall communicate to the legislature at each regular session each case of remission of fine, reprieve, commutation or pardon granted by him, stating the name of the convict, the crime for which he was convicted, the sentence and its date, and the date of the remission, commutation, pardon or reprieve with his reasons for granting the same.

Section 6. Acting Governor

If the governor be impeached, displaced, resign or die, or from mental or physical disease or otherwise become incapable of performing the duties of his office or be absent from the state, the secretary of state shall act as governor until the vacancy is filled or the disability removed.

Section 7. When Governor may Fill Vacancies in Office

When any office from any cause becomes vacant, and no mode is provided by the constitution or law for filling such vacancy, the governor shall have the power to fill the same by appointment.

Section 8. Approval or Veto of Legislation by Governor; Passage Over Veto

Every bill which has passed the legislature shall, before it becomes a law, be presented to the governor. If he approve, he shall sign it; but if not, he shall return it with his objections to the house in which it originated, which shall enter the objections at large upon the journal and proceed to reconsider it. If, after such reconsideration, two-thirds of the members elected agree to pass the bill, it shall be sent, together with the objections, to the other house, by which it shall likewise be reconsidered, and if it be approved by two-thirds of the members elected, it shall become a law; but in all such cases the vote of both houses shall be determined by the yeas and nays, and the names of the members voting for and against the bill shall be entered upon the journal of each house respectively. If any bill is not returned by the governor within three days (Sundays excepted) after its presentation to him, the same shall be a law, unless the legislature by its adjournment, prevent its return, in which case it shall be a law, unless he shall file the same with his objections in the office of the secretary of state within fifteen days after such adjournment.

Section 9. Veto of Items of Appropriations

The governor shall have power to disapprove of any item or items or part or parts of any bill making appropriations of money or property embracing distinct items, and the part or parts of the bill approved shall be the law, and the item or items and part or parts disapproved shall be void unless enacted in the following manner: If the legislature be in session he shall transmit to the house in which the bill originated a copy of the item or items or part or parts thereof disapproved, together with his objections thereto, and the items or parts objected to shall be separately reconsidered, and each item or part shall then take the same course as is prescribed for the passage of bills over the executive veto.

Section 10. Bribery or Coercion of or by Governor

Any governor of this state who asks, receives or agrees to receive any bribe upon any understanding that his official opinion, judgment or action shall be influenced thereby, or who gives or offers, or promises his official influence in consideration that any member of the legislature shall give his official vote or influence on any particular side of any question or matter upon which he is required to act in his official capacity, or who menaces any member by the threatened use of his veto power, or who offers or promises any member that he, the governor, will appoint any particular person or persons to any office created or thereafter to be created, in consideration that any member shall give his official vote or influence on any matter pending or thereafter to be introduced into either house of said legislature; or who threatens any member that he, the governor, will remove any person or persons from office or position with intent in any manner to influence the action of said members, shall be punished in the manner now or that may hereafter be provided by law, and upon conviction thereof shall forfeit all right to hold or exercise any office of trust or honor in this state.

Section 11. State Officers; Election; Qualifications; Terms

There shall be chosen by the qualified electors of the state at the times and places of choosing members of the legislature, a secretary of state, auditor, treasurer, and superintendent of public instruction, who shall have attained the age of twenty-five (25) years respectively, shall be citizens of the United States, and shall have the qualifications of state electors. They shall severally hold their offices at the seat of government, for the term of four (4) years and until their successors are elected and duly qualified. The legislature may provide for such other state officers as are deemed necessary.

Section 12. State Officers; Powers and Duties

The powers and duties of the secretary of state, of state auditor, treasurer and superintendent of public instruction shall be as prescribed by law.

Section 13. Salaries of Governor and Other Elective State Officers

Until otherwise provided by law, the governor shall receive an annual salary of two thousand and five hundred dollars, the secretary of state, state auditor, state treasurer and superintendent of public instruction shall each receive an annual salary of two thousand dollars, and the salaries of any of the said officers shall not be increased or diminished during the period for which they were elected, and all fees and profits arising from any of the said offices shall be covered into the state treasury.

Section 14. Examination of Accounts

The legislature shall provide by law for examination of the accounts of state treasurer, supreme court clerks, district court clerks, and all county treasurers, and treasurers of such other public institutions as the legislature may prescribe. This section was amended by a resolution adopted by the 1989 legislature, ratified by a vote of the people at the general election held on November 6, 1990, and proclaimed in effect on November 28, 1990. Section 15. Great seal of state. There shall be a seal of state which shall be called the "Great Seal of the State of Wyoming"; it shall be kept by the secretary of state and used by him officially as directed by law. The seal of the Territory of Wyoming as now used shall be the seal of the state until otherwise provided by law.

ARTICLE 5. JUDICIAL DEPARTMENT

Section 1. How Judicial Power Vested

The judicial power of the state shall be vested in the senate, sitting as a court of impeachment, in a supreme court, district courts, and such subordinate courts as the legislature may, by general law, establish and ordain from time to time.

Section 2. Supreme Court Generally; Appellate Jurisdiction

The supreme court shall have general appellate jurisdiction, co-extensive with the state, in both civil and criminal causes, and shall have a general superintending control over all inferior courts, under such rules and regulations as may be prescribed by law.

Section 3. Supreme Court Generally; Original Jurisdiction

The supreme court shall have original jurisdiction in quo warranto and mandamus as to all state officers, and in habeas corpus. The supreme court shall also have power to issue writs of mandamus, review, prohibition, habeas corpus, certiorari, and other writs necessary and proper to the complete exercise of its appellate and revisory jurisdiction. Each of the judges shall have power to issue writs of habeas corpus to any part of the state upon petition by or on behalf of a person held in actual custody, and may make such writs returnable before himself or before the supreme court, or before any district court of the state or any judge thereof.

Section 4. Supreme Court Generally; Number; Election of Chief Justice; Quorum; Vacancies in Supreme Court or District Court; Judicial Nominating Commission; Terms; Standing for Retention in Office

(a) The supreme court of the state shall consist of not less than three nor more than five justices as may be determined by the legislature. The justices of the court shall elect one of their number to serve as chief justice for such term and with such authority as shall be prescribed by law. A majority of the justices shall constitute a quorum, and a concurrence of a majority of such quorum shall be sufficient to decide any matter. If a justice of the supreme court for any reason shall not participate in hearing any matter, the chief justice may designate one of the district judges to act for such nonparticipating justice.

(b) A vacancy in the office of justice of the supreme court or judge of any district court or of such other courts that may be made subject to this provision by law, shall be filled by a qualified person appointed by the governor from a list of three nominees that shall be submitted by the judicial nominating commission. The commission shall submit such a list not later than 60 days after the death, retirement, tender of resignation, removal, failure of an incumbent to file a declaration of candidacy or certification of a negative majority vote on the question of retention in office under section [subsection] (g) hereof. If the governor shall fail to make any such appointment within 30 days from the day the list is submitted to him, such appointment shall be made by the chief justice from the list within 15 days.

(c) There shall be a judicial nominating commission for the supreme court, district courts and any other courts to which these provisions may be extended by law. The commission shall consist of seven members, one of whom shall be the chief justice, or a justice of the supreme court designated by the chief justice to act for him, who shall be chairman thereof. In addition to the chief justice, or his designee, three resident members of the bar engaged in active practice shall be elected by the Wyoming state bar and three electors of the state not admitted to practice law shall be appointed by the governor to serve on said commission for such staggered terms as shall be prescribed by law. No more than two members of said commission who are residents of the same judicial district may qualify to serve any term or part of a term on the commission. In the case of courts having less than statewide authority, each judicial district not otherwise represented by a member on the commission, and each county, should the provisions hereof be extended by law to courts of lesser jurisdiction than district courts, shall be represented by two nonvoting advisers to the commission when an appointment to a court in such unrepresented district, or county, is pending; both of such advisers shall be residents of the district, or county, and one shall be a member of the bar appointed by the governing body of the Wyoming state bar and one shall be a non-attorney advisor appointed by the governor.

(d) No member of the commission excepting the chairman shall hold any federal, state or county public office or any political party office, and after serving a full term he shall not be eligible for reelection or reappointment to succeed himself on the commission. No member of the judicial nominating commission shall be eligible for appointment to any judicial office while he is a member of the commission nor for a period of one year after the expiration of his term for which he was elected or appointed. Vacancies in the office of commissioner shall be filled for the unexpired terms in the same manner as the original appointments. Additional qualifications of members of the commission may be prescribed by law.

(e) The chairman of the commission shall cast votes only in the event of ties. The commission shall operate under rules adopted by the supreme court. Members of the commission shall be entitled to no compensation other than expenses incurred for travel and subsistence while attending meetings of the commission.

(f) The terms of supreme court justices shall be eight years and the terms of district court judges shall be six years.

(g) Each justice or judge selected under these provisions shall serve for one year after his appointment and until the first Monday in January following the next general election after the expiration of such year. He shall, at such general election, stand for retention in office on a ballot which shall submit to the appropriate electorate the question whether such justice or judge shall be retained in office for another term or part of a term, and upon filing a declaration of candidacy in the form and at the times prescribed by law, he shall, at the general election next held before the expiration of each term, stand for retention on such ballots. The electorate of the whole state shall vote on the question of retention or rejection of justices of the supreme court, and any other statewide court; the electorate of the several judicial districts shall vote on the question of retention or rejection of judges of their respective districts, and the electorate of such other subdivisions of the state as shall be prescribed by law shall vote on the question of retention or rejection of any other judges to which these provisions may be extended.

(h) A justice or judge selected hereunder, or one that is in office upon the effective date of this amendment, who shall desire to retain his judicial office a succeeding term, following the expiration of his existing term of office, shall file with the appropriate office not more than 6 months nor less than 3 months before the general election to be held before the expiration of his existing term of office a declaration of intent to stand for election for a succeeding term. When such a declaration of intent is filed, the appropriate electorate shall vote upon a nonpartisan judicial ballot on the question of retention in or rejection from office of such justice or judge, and if a majority of those voting on the question vote affirmatively, the justice or judge shall be elected to serve the succeeding term prescribed by law. If a justice or judge fails to file such a declaration within the time specified, or if a majority of those voting on the question vote negatively to any judicial candidacy, a vacancy will thereby be created in that office at the end of its existing term.

Section 5. Voluntary Retirement and Compensation of Justices and Judges

Subject to the further provisions of this section, the legislature shall provide for the voluntary retirement and compensation of justices and judges of the supreme court and district courts, and may do so for any other courts, on account of length of service, age and disability, and for their reassignment to active duty where and when needed. The office of every such justice and judge shall become vacant when the incumbent reaches the age of seventy (70) years, as the legislature may prescribe; but, in the case of an incumbent whose term of office includes the effective date of this amendment, this provision shall not prevent him from serving the remainder of said term nor be applicable to him before his period or periods of judicial service shall have reached a total of six (6) years. The legislature may also provide for benefits for dependents of justices and judges.

Section 6. Commission on Judicial Conduct and Ethics

(a) There is hereby created the Commission on Judicial Conduct and Ethics. The commission shall have twelve (12) members who reside in Wyoming consisting of:

(i) Three (3) active Wyoming judges, who are not members of the supreme court, elected by the full-time, active Wyoming judges;

(ii) Three (3) members of the Wyoming state bar, appointed by its governing body; and

(iii) Six (6) electors of the state, who are not active or retired judges, or attorneys, appointed by the governor and confirmed by the senate.

(b) All terms shall be for three (3) years duration. Members shall be eligible for reappointment to a second term.

(c) The commission shall divide itself into investigatory and adjudicatory panels for each case considered. No commission member may serve on an adjudicatory panel in any case in which that member served in an investigatory capacity.

(d) The commission, or a panel thereof, shall consider complaints of judicial misconduct made against judicial officers and, to the extent permitted and as provided for by the code of judicial conduct, may:

(i) Discipline a judicial officer; or

(ii) Recommend discipline of a judicial officer to the supreme court or a special supreme court. **(e)** The supreme court shall adopt a code of judicial conduct applicable to all judicial officers and adopt rules governing:

(i) The election of judges to the commission;

(ii) The staggering of terms, and the removal and filling of vacancies of commission members;

(iii) The appointment of a special supreme court composed of five (5) district judges who are not members of the commission, to act in the place of the supreme court in any case involving the discipline or disability of a justice of the supreme court; and

(iv) Procedures for the operation of the commission including exercise of the commission's disciplinary powers.

(f) The supreme court or special supreme court, on recommendation of the commission or on its own motion may:

(i) Suspend a judicial officer without salary when the judicial officer is charged with or is convicted in the United States of a crime punishable as a felony or one involving moral turpitude under Wyoming or federal law, and remove that judicial officer in the event such conviction becomes final;

(ii) For any judicial officer removed from office, order a forfeiture of any pension or retirement benefits accrued after the offending conduct, except for those that have been vested under the Wyoming retirement act or any local plan;

(iii) Suspend the judicial officer from practicing law in this state; and

(iv) Remove a judicial officer from office or impose other discipline permitted by the rules for judicial discipline for conduct that constitutes willful misconduct in office, or for a willful and persistent failure to perform the duties of the office, or for habitual intemperance, or for conduct prejudicial to the administration of justice that brings the judicial office into disrepute, or for a violation of the code of judicial conduct.

(g) The code of judicial conduct shall provide for the mandatory retirement of a judicial officer for any disability that seriously interferes with the performance of the duties of the office and is, or is likely to become, permanent. A judicial officer retired by the supreme court or a special supreme court for a disability shall be considered to have retired voluntarily without loss of retirement benefits.

(h) A judicial officer removed from office is ineligible for any judicial office.

(j) This section applies to all judicial officers during their service on the bench and to former judicial officers regarding allegations of judicial misconduct occurring during service on the bench if a complaint is made within one (1) year following service. The term "judicial officer" includes all members of the judicial branch of government performing judicial functions.

Section 7. Supreme Court Generally; Terms of Court

At least two terms of the supreme court shall be held annually at the seat of government at such times as may be provided by law.

Section 8. Supreme Court Generally; Qualifications of Justices

No person shall be eligible to the office of justice of the supreme court unless he be learned in the law, have been in actual practice at least nine (9) years, or whose service on the bench of any court of record, when added to the time he may have practiced law, shall be equal to nine (9) years, be at least thirty years of age and a citizen of the United States, nor unless he shall have resided in this state or territory at least three years.

Section 9. Supreme Court Generally; Clerk

There shall be a clerk of the supreme court who shall be appointed by the justices of said court and shall hold his office during their pleasure, and whose duties and emoluments shall be as provided by law.

Section 10. District Courts Generally; Jurisdiction

The district court shall have original jurisdiction of all causes both at law and in equity and in all criminal cases, of all matters of probate and insolvency and of such special cases and proceedings as are not otherwise provided for. The district court shall also have original jurisdiction in all cases and of all proceedings in which jurisdiction shall not have been by law vested exclusively in some other court; and said court shall have the power of naturalization and to issue papers therefor. They shall have such appellate jurisdiction in cases arising in justices' and other inferior courts in their respective counties as may be prescribed by law. Said courts and their judges shall have power to issue writs of mandamus, quo warranto, review, certiorari, prohibition, injunction and writs of habeas corpus, on petition by or on behalf of any person in actual custody in their respective districts.

Section 11. District Courts Generally; Judges to Hold Court for Each Other

The judges of the district courts may hold courts for each other and shall do so when required by law.

Section 12. District Courts Generally; Qualifications of Judges

No person shall be eligible to the office of judge of the district court unless he be learned in the law, be at least twenty-eight years of age, and a citizen of the United States, nor unless he shall have resided within the State or Territory of Wyoming at least two years next preceding his election.

Section 13. District Courts Generally; Clerks

There shall be a clerk of the district court in each organized county in which a court is holden who shall be elected, or, in case of vacancy, appointed in such manner and with such duties and compensation as may be prescribed by law.

Section 14. District Courts Generally; Commissioners

The legislature shall provide by law for the appointment by the several district courts of one or more district court commissioners (who shall be persons learned in the law) in each organized county in which a district court is holden, such commissioners shall have authority to perform such chamber business in the absence of the district judge from the county or upon his written statement filed with the papers, that it is improper for him to act, as may be prescribed by law, to take depositions and perform such other duties, and receive such compensation as shall be prescribed by law.

Section 15. Style of Process

The style of all process shall be "The State of Wyoming." All prosecutions shall be carried on in the name and by the authority of the State of Wyoming, and conclude "against the peace and dignity of the State of Wyoming."

Section 16. Supreme Court Judges Limited to Judicial Duties

No duties shall be imposed by law upon the supreme court or any of the judges thereof, except such as are judicial, nor shall any of the judges thereof exercise any power of appointment except as herein provided.

Section 17. Salaries of Judges of Supreme and District Courts

The judges of the supreme and district courts shall receive such compensation for their services as may be prescribed by law, which compensation shall not be increased or diminished during the term for which a judge shall have been elected, and the salary of a judge of the supreme or district court shall be as may be prescribed by law; provided, however, that when any legislative increase or decrease in the salary of the justices or judges of such courts whose respective terms of office do not expire at the same time, has heretofore or shall hereafter become effective as to any member of such court, it shall be effective from such date as to each of the members thereof.

Section 18. Appeals from District Courts to Supreme Court

Writs of error and appeals may be allowed from the decisions of the district courts to the supreme court under such regulations as may be prescribed by law.

Section 19. State Divided Into Districts; Election and Terms of District Judges

Until otherwise provided by law, the state shall be divided into three judicial districts, in each of which there shall be elected at general elections, by the electors thereof, one judge of the district court therein, whose term shall be six (6) years from the first Monday in January succeeding his election and until his successor is duly qualified.

Section 20. Districts Defined

Until otherwise provided by law, said judicial districts shall be constituted as follows: District number one shall consist of the counties of Laramie, Converse and Crook. District number two shall consist of the counties of Albany, Johnson and Sheridan. District number three shall consist of the counties of Carbon, Sweetwater, Uinta and Fremont.

Section 21. Increase in Number of Districts and Judges

The legislature may from time to time increase the number of said judicial districts and the judges thereof, but such increase or change in the boundaries of the district shall not work the removal of any judge from his office during the term for which he may have been elected or appointed; provided the number of districts and district judges shall not exceed four (4) until the valuation of taxable property in the state shall be equal to one hundred million ($100,000,000) dollars.

Section 22. Jurisdiction of Justices of the Peace

Repealed

Section 23. Appeals From Justices Courts

Repealed

Section 24. Terms of District Courts; Attaching Unorganized Territory to Organized Counties

The time of holding courts in the several counties of a district shall be as prescribed by law, and the legislature shall make provisions for attaching unorganized counties or territory to organized counties for judicial purposes.

Section 25. Judges of Supreme and District Courts Shall Not Practice

No judge of the supreme or district court shall act as attorney or counsellor at law.

Section 26. Power to Fix Terms of Court

Until the legislature shall provide by law for fixing the terms of courts, the judges of the supreme court and district courts shall fix the terms thereof.

Section 27. Judges of Supreme and District Courts Shall Not Hold Other Office

No judge of the supreme or district court shall be elected or appointed to any other than judicial offices or be eligible thereto during the term for which he was elected or appointed such judge.

Section 28. Appeals from Boards of Arbitration

Appeals from decisions of compulsory boards of arbitration shall be allowed to the supreme court of the state, and the manner of taking such appeals shall be prescribed by law.

Section 29. Juvenile Delinquency and Domestic Relations Courts

The legislature may by general law provide for such juvenile delinquency and domestic relations courts as may be needed, and for the number, qualifications and election of judges of such courts. Appeals shall lie in such cases and pursuant to such regulations as may be prescribed by law. Such courts shall have such jurisdiction as the legislature may by law provide.

ARTICLE 6. SUFFRAGE AND ELECTIONS

Section 1. Male and Female Citizens to Enjoy Equal Rights

The rights of citizens of the State of Wyoming to vote and hold office shall not be denied or abridged on account of sex. Both male and female citizens of this state shall equally enjoy all civil, political and religious rights and privileges. Wyoming was the first state in the Union to grant women equal suffrage with men.

Section 2. Qualifications of Electors

Every citizen of the United States of the age of twenty-one years and upwards, who has resided in the state or territory one year and in the county wherein such residence is located sixty days next preceding any election, shall be entitled to vote at such election, except as herein otherwise provided.

Section 3. Electors Privileged From Arrest

Electors shall in all cases except treason, felony or breach of the peace, be privileged from arrest on the days of election during their attendance at elections, and going to and returning therefrom.

Section 4. Exemption of Electors From Military Duty

No elector shall be obliged to perform militia duty on the day of election, except in time of war or public danger.

Section 5. Electors Must be Citizens of United States

No person shall be deemed a qualified elector of this state, unless such person be a citizen of the United States.

Section 6. What Persons Excluded From Franchise

All persons adjudicated to be mentally incompetent or persons convicted of felonies, unless restored to civil rights, are excluded from the elective franchise.

Section 7. When Residence not Lost by Reason of Absence

No elector shall be deemed to have lost his residence in the state, by reason of his absence on business of the United States, or of this state, or in the military or naval service of the United States.

Section 8. Soldiers Stationed in State not Considered Residents

No soldier, seaman, or marine in the army or navy of the United States shall be deemed a resident of this state in consequence of his being stationed therein.

Section 9. Educational Qualifications of Electors

No person shall have the right to vote who shall not be able to read the constitution of this state.

Section 10. Alien Suffrage

Nothing herein contained shall be construed to deprive any person of the right to vote who has such right at the time of the adoption of this constitution, unless disqualified by the restrictions of section six of this article. After the expiration of five (5) years from the time of the adoption of this constitution, none but citizens of the United States shall have the right to vote.

Section 11. Manner of Holding Elections

All elections shall be by ballot. The legislature shall provide by law that the names of all candidates for the same office, to be voted for at any election, shall be printed on the same ballot, at public expense, and on election day be delivered to the voters within the polling place by sworn public officials, and only such ballots so delivered shall be received and counted. But no voter shall be deprived the privilege of writing upon the ballot used the name of any other candidate. All voters shall be guaranteed absolute privacy in the preparation of their ballots, and the secrecy of the ballot shall be made compulsory.

Section 12. Registration of Voters Required

No person qualified to be an elector of the State of Wyoming, shall be allowed to vote at any general or special election hereafter to be holden in the state, until he or she shall have registered as a voter according to law, unless the failure to register is caused by sickness or absence, for which provisions shall be made by law. The legislature of the state shall enact such laws as will carry into effect the provisions of this section, which enactment shall be subject to amendment, but shall never be repealed; but this section shall not apply to the first election held under this constitution.

Section 13. Purity of Elections to be Provided For

The legislature shall pass laws to secure the purity of elections, and guard against abuses of the elective franchise.

Section 14. Election Contests

The legislature shall, by general law, designate the courts by which the several classes of election contests not otherwise provided for, shall be tried, and regulate the manner of trial and all matters incident thereto; but no such law shall apply to any contest arising out of an election held before its passage.

Section 15. Qualifications for Office

No person except a qualified elector shall be elected or appointed to any civil or military office in the state. "Military office" shall be limited to the offices of adjutant general, assistant adjutant general for the army national guard and assistant adjutant general for the air national guard.

Section 16. When Officers to Hold Over; Suspension of Officers

Every person holding any civil office under the state or any municipality therein shall, unless removed according to law, exercise the duties of such office until his successor is duly qualified, but this shall not apply to members of the legislature, nor to members of any board or assembly, two or more of whom are elected at the same time. The legislature may by law provide for suspending any officer in his functions, pending impeachment or prosecution for misconduct in office.

Section 17. Time of Holding General and Special Elections; When Elected Officers to Enter Upon Duties

All general elections for state and county officers, for members of the house of representatives and the senate of the State of Wyoming, and representatives to the congress of the United States, shall be held on the Tuesday next following the first Monday in November of each even year. Special elections may be held as now, or may hereafter be provided by law. All state and county officers elected at a general election shall enter upon their respective duties on the first Monday in January next following the date of their election, or as soon thereafter as may be possible.

Section 18. Method of Selecting Officers Whose Election is not Provided For

All officers, whose election is not provided for in this constitution, shall be elected or appointed as may be directed by law.

Section 19. Dual Office Holding

No member of congress from this state, nor any person holding or exercising any office or appointment of trust or profit under the United States, shall at the same time hold or exercise any office in this state to which a salary, fees or perquisites shall be attached. The legislature may by law declare what offices are incompatible.

Section 20. Oath of Office; Form

Senators and representatives and all judicial, state and county officers shall, before entering on the duties of their respective offices, take and subscribe the following oath or affirmation: "I do solemnly swear (or affirm) that I will support, obey and defend the constitution of the United States, and the constitution of the state of Wyoming; that I have not knowingly violated any law related to my election or appointment, or caused it to be done by others; and that I will discharge the duties of my office with fidelity."

Section 21. Oath of Office; How Administered

The foregoing oath shall be administered by some person authorized to administer oaths, and in the case of state officers and judges of the supreme court shall be filed in the office of the secretary of state, and in the case of other judicial and county officers in the office of the clerk of the county in which the same is taken; any person refusing to take said oath or affirmation shall forfeit his office, and any person who shall be convicted of having sworn or affirmed falsely, or of having violated said oath or affirmation, shall be guilty of perjury, and be forever disqualified from holding any office of trust or profit within this state. The oath to members of the senate and house of representatives shall be administered by one of the judges of the supreme court or a justice of the peace, in the hall of the house to which the members shall be elected.

Section 22. Absent Voter Ballots, Voting and Registration

The provisions of section 11 of article 6 of this constitution, which provides that the ballots therein mentioned shall be delivered on election day to the voters within the polling place by sworn public officials, and that only such ballots so delivered shall be received and counted, shall not be applicable to, affect or invalidate absent voter ballots and voting thereof and registration therefor, as provided by article 14, of chapter 36, Wyoming Revised Statutes, 1931, and other acts of the legislature of the State of Wyoming, amendatory thereof or related thereto, whether heretofore or hereafter enacted.

ARTICLE 7. EDUCATION; STATE INSTITUTIONS; PROMOTION OF HEALTH AND MORALS; PUBLIC BUILDINGS

Section 1. Legislature to Provide for Public Schools

The legislature shall provide for the establishment and maintenance of a complete and uniform system of public instruction, embracing free elementary schools of every needed kind and grade, a university with such technical and professional departments as the public good may require and the means of the state allow, and such other institutions as may be necessary.

Section 2. School Revenues

The following are declared to be perpetual funds for school purposes, of which the annual income only can be appropriated, to wit: Such per centum as has been or may hereafter be granted by congress on the sale of lands in this state; all moneys arising from the sale or lease of sections number sixteen and thirty-six in each township in the state, and the lands selected or that may be selected in lieu thereof; the proceeds of all lands that have been or may hereafter be granted to this state, where by the terms and conditions of the grant, the same are not to be otherwise appropriated; the net proceeds of lands and other property and effects that may come to the state by escheat or forfeiture, or from unclaimed dividends or distributive shares of the estates of deceased persons; all moneys, stocks, bonds, lands and other property now belonging to the common school funds. Provided, that the rents for the ordinary use of said lands shall be applied to the support of public schools and, when authorized by general law, not to exceed thirty-three and one-third (33 1/3) per centum of oil, gas, coal, or other mineral royalties arising from the lease of any said school lands may be so applied.

Section 3. Other Sources of School Revenues

To the sources of revenue above mentioned shall be added all other grants, gifts and devises that have been or may hereafter be made to this state and not otherwise appropriated by the terms of the grant, gift or devise.

Section 4. Restriction in Use of Revenues

All money, stocks, bonds, lands and other property belonging to a county school fund, except such moneys and property as may be provided by law for current use in aid of public schools, shall belong to and be invested by the several counties as a county public school fund, in such manner as the legislature shall by law provide, the income of which shall be appropriated exclusively to the use and support of free public schools in the several counties of the state.

Section 5. Fines and Penalties to Belong to Public School Fund

All fines and penalties under general laws of the state shall belong to the public school fund of the respective counties and be paid over to the custodians of such funds for the current support of the public schools therein.

Section 6. State to Keep School Funds; Investment

All funds belonging to the state for public school purposes, the interest and income of which only are to be used, shall be deemed trust funds in the care of the state, which shall keep them for the exclusive benefit of the public schools. The legislature shall provide by law for the investment of such trust funds.

Section 7. Application of School Funds

The income arising from the funds mentioned in the preceding section, together with all the rents of the unsold school lands and such other means as the legislature may provide, shall be exclusively applied to the support of free schools in every county in the state.

Section 8. Distribution of School Funds

Provision shall be made by general law for the equitable allocation of such income among all school districts in the state. But no appropriation shall be made from said fund to any district for the year in which a school has not been maintained for at least three (3) months; nor shall any portion of any public school fund ever be used to support or assist any private school, or any school, academy, seminary, college or other institution of learning controlled by any church or sectarian organization or religious denomination whatsoever.

Section 9. Taxation for Schools

The legislature shall make such further provision by taxation or otherwise, as with the income arising from the general school fund will create and maintain a thorough and efficient system of public schools, adequate to the proper instruction of all youth of the state, between the ages of six and twenty-one years, free of charge; and in view of such provision so made, the legislature shall require that every child of sufficient physical and mental ability shall attend a public school during the period between six and eighteen years for a time equivalent to three years, unless educated by other means.

Section 10. No Discrimination Between Pupils

In none of the public schools so established and maintained shall distinction or discrimination be made on account of sex, race or color.

Section 11. Textbooks

Neither the legislature nor the superintendent of public instruction shall have power to prescribe text books to be used in the public schools.

Section 12. Sectarianism Prohibited

No sectarian instruction, qualifications or tests shall be imparted, exacted, applied or in any manner tolerated in the schools of any grade or character controlled by the state, nor shall attendance be required at any religious service therein, nor shall any sectarian tenets or doctrines be taught or favored in any public school or institution that may be established under this constitution.

Section 13. Land Commissioners

Superseded

Section 14. Supervision of Schools Entrusted to State Superintendent of Public Instruction

The general supervision of the public schools shall be entrusted to the state superintendent of public instruction, whose powers and duties shall be prescribed by law.

Section 15. Establishment of University Confirmed

The establishment of the University of Wyoming is hereby confirmed, and said institution, with its several departments, is hereby declared to be the University of the State of Wyoming. All lands which have been heretofore granted or which may be granted hereafter by congress unto the university as such, or in aid of the instruction to be given in any of its departments, with all other grants, donations, or devises for said university, or for any of its departments, shall vest in said university, and be exclusively used for the purposes for which they were granted, donated or devised. The said lands may be leased on terms approved by the land commissioners, but may not be sold on terms not approved by congress.

Section 16. Tuition Free

The university shall be equally open to students of both sexes, irrespective of race or color; and, in order that the instruction furnished may be as nearly free as possible, any amount in addition to the income from its grants of lands and other sources above mentioned, necessary to its support and maintenance in a condition of full efficiency shall be raised by taxation or otherwise, under provisions of the legislature.

Section 17. Government of University

The legislature shall provide by law for the management of the university, its lands and other property by a board of trustees, consisting of not less than seven members, to be appointed by the governor by and with the advice and consent of the senate, and the president of the university, and the superintendent of public instruction, as members ex officio, as such having the right to speak, but not to vote. The duties and powers of the trustees shall be prescribed by law.

Section 18. Establishment; Supervision by State Board of Charities and Reform

Such charitable, reformatory and penal institutions as the claims of humanity and the public good may require, shall be established and supported by the state in such manner as the legislature may prescribe. They shall be supervised as prescribed by law.

Section 19. Territorial Institutions Pass to State

The property of all charitable and penal institutions belonging to the Territory of Wyoming shall, upon the adoption of this constitution, become the property of the State of Wyoming, and such of said institutions as are then in actual operation, shall thereafter have the supervision of the board of charities and reform as provided in the last preceding section of this article, under provisions of the legislature.

Section 20. Duty of Legislature to Protect and Promote Health and Morality of People

As the health and morality of the people are essential to their well-being, and to the peace and permanence of the state, it shall be the duty of the legislature to protect and promote these vital interests by such measures for the encouragement of temperance and virtue, and such restrictions upon vice and immorality of every sort, as are deemed necessary to the public welfare.

Section 21. Buildings and Property of Territory Pass to State

All public buildings and other property, belonging to the territory shall, upon the adoption of this constitution, become the property of the State of Wyoming.

Section 22. Construction and Supervision

The construction, care and preservation of all public buildings of the state not under the control of the board or officers of public institutions by authority of law shall be entrusted to such officers or boards, and under such regulations as shall be prescribed by law.

Section 23. Permanent Location

The legislature shall have no power to change or to locate the seat of government, the state university, or state hospital, but may provide by law for submitting the question of the permanent locations thereof respectively, to the qualified electors of the state, at some general election, and a majority of all votes upon said question cast at said election, shall be necessary to determine the location thereof; but until the same are respectively and permanently located, as herein provided, the location of the seat of government and said institutions shall be as follows: The seat of government shall be located at the City of Cheyenne, in the County of Laramie. The state university shall be centered at the City of Laramie, in the County of Albany. The state hospital shall be located at or near the City of Evanston, in the County of Uinta. A penitentiary shall be located at or near the City of Rawlins, in the County of Carbon. The legislature may provide by law the location of other public institutions, including correctional facilities.

ARTICLE 8. IRRIGATION AND WATER RIGHTS

Section 1. Water is State Property

The water of all natural streams, springs, lakes or other collections of still water, within the boundaries of the state, are hereby declared to be the property of the state.

Section 2. Board of Control

There shall be constituted a board of control, to be composed of the state engineer and superintendents of the water divisions; which shall, under such regulations as may be prescribed by law, have the supervision of the waters of the state and of their appropriation, distribution and diversion, and of the various officers connected therewith. Its decisions to be subject to review by the courts of the state.

Section 3. Priority of Appropriation

Priority of appropriation for beneficial uses shall give the better right. No appropriation shall be denied except when such denial is demanded by the public interests.

Section 4. Water Divisions

The legislature shall by law divide the state into four (4) water divisions, and provide for the appointment of superintendents thereof.

Section 5. State Engineer

There shall be a state engineer who shall be appointed by the governor of the state and confirmed by the senate; he shall hold his office for the term of six (6) years, or until his successor shall have been appointed and shall have qualified. He shall be president of the board of control, and shall have general supervision of the waters of the state and of the officers connected with its distribution. No person shall be appointed to this position who has not such theoretical knowledge and such practical experience and skill as shall fit him for the position.

ARTICLE 9. MINES AND MINING

Section 1. Inspector of Mines

There shall be established and maintained the office of inspector of mines, the duties of which shall be prescribed by law.

Section 2. Legislature to Enact Regulatory Laws

The legislature shall provide by law for the proper development, ventilation, drainage and operation of all mines in this state.

Section 3. Restrictions on Employment in Mines

Repealed

Section 4. Right of Action for Injuries

For any injury to person or property caused by wilful failure to comply with the provisions of this article, or laws passed in pursuance hereof, a right of action shall accrue to the party injured, for the damage sustained thereby, and in all cases in this state, whenever the death of a person shall be caused by wrongful act, neglect or default, such as would, if death had not ensued, have entitled the party injured to maintain an action to recover damages in respect thereof, the person who, or the corporation which would have been liable, if death had not ensued, shall be liable to an action for damages notwithstanding the death of the person injured, and the legislature shall provide by law at its first session for the manner in which the right of action in respect thereto shall be enforced.

Section 5. School of Mines

The legislature may provide that the science of mining and metallurgy be taught in one of the institutions of learning under the patronage of the state.

Section 6. State Geologist

Repealed

ARTICLE 10. CORPORATIONS

Section 1. Creation

The legislature shall provide for the organization of corporations by general law. All laws relating to corporations may be altered, amended or repealed by the legislature at any time when necessary for the public good and general welfare, and all corporations doing business in this state may as to such business be regulated, limited or restrained by law not in conflict with the constitution of the United States.

Section 2. Control by State

All powers and franchises of corporations are derived from the people and are granted by their agent, the government, for the public good and general welfare, and the right and duty of the state to control and regulate them for these purposes is hereby declared. The power, rights and privileges of any and all corporations may be forfeited by willful neglect or abuse thereof. The police power of the state is supreme over all corporations as well as individuals.

Section 3. Forfeited Charters

Executed

Section 4. Damages for Personal Injuries or Death; Worker's Compensation

(a) No law shall be enacted limiting the amount of damages to be recovered for causing the injury or death of any person.

(b) Any section of this constitution to the contrary notwithstanding, for any civil action where a person alleges that a health care provider's act or omission in the provision of health care resulted in death or injury, the legislature may by general law:

(i) Mandate alternative dispute resolution or review by a medical review panel before the filing of a civil action against the health care provider.

(c) Any contract or agreement with any employee waiving any right to recover damages for causing the death or injury of any employee shall be void. As to all extra-hazardous employments the legislature shall provide by law for the accumulation and maintenance of a fund or funds out of which shall be paid compensation as may be fixed by law according to proper classifications to each person injured in such employment or to the dependent families of such as die as the result of such injuries, except in case of injuries due solely to the culpable negligence of the injured employee. The fund or funds shall be accumulated, paid into the state treasury and maintained in such manner as may be provided by law. Monies in the fund shall be expended only for compensation authorized by this section, for administration and management of the Worker's Compensation Act, debt service related to the fund and for workplace safety programs conducted by the state as authorized by law. The right of each employee to compensation from the fund shall be in lieu of and shall take the place of any and all rights of action against any employer contributing as required by law to the fund in favor of any person or persons by reason of the injuries or death. Subject to conditions specified by law, the legislature may allow employments not designated extra-hazardous to be covered by the state fund at the option of the employer. To the extent an employer elects to be covered by the state fund and contributes to the fund as required by law, the employer shall enjoy the same immunity as provided for extra-hazardous employments.

Section 5. Acceptance of Constitution

No corporation organized under the laws of Wyoming Territory or any other jurisdiction than this state, shall be permitted to transact business in this state until it shall have accepted the constitution of this state and filed such acceptance in accordance with the laws thereof.

Section 6. Engaging in More Than One Line of Business

Corporations shall have power to engage in such and as many lines or departments of business as the legislature shall provide.

Section 7. What Corporations are Common Carriers

All corporations engaged in the transportation of persons, property, mineral oils, and minerals products, news or intelligence, including railroads, telegraphs, express companies, pipe lines and telephones, are declared to be common carriers.

Section 8. Trusts Prohibited

There shall be no consolidation or combination of corporations of any kind whatever to prevent competition, to control or influence productions or prices thereof, or in any other manner to interfere with the public good and general welfare.

Section 9. Eminent Domain

The right of eminent domain shall never be so abridged or construed as to prevent the legislature from taking property and franchises of incorporated companies and subjecting them to public use the same as the property of individuals.

Section 10. Mutual and Co-Operative associations

The legislature shall provide by suitable legislation for the organization of mutual and cooperative associations or corporations.

Section 11. Powers and Rights of Railroads

Any railroad corporation or association organized for the purpose, shall have the right to construct and operate a railroad between any points within this state and to connect at the state line with railroads of other states. Every railroad shall have the right with its road to intersect, connect with or cross any other railroad, and all railroads shall receive and transport each other's passengers, and tonnage and cars, loaded or empty, without delay or discrimination.

Section 12. Discrimination by Railroads and Telegraph Lines Forbidden

Railroad and telegraph lines heretofore constructed or that may hereafter be constructed in this state are hereby declared public highways and common carriers, and as such must be made by law to extend the same equality and impartiality to all who use them, excepting employees and their families and ministers of the gospel, whether individuals or corporations.

Section 13. Railroads to Make Annual Reports to State Auditor

Every railroad corporation or association operating a line of railroad within this state shall annually make a report to the auditor of state of its business within this state, in such form as the legislature may prescribe.

Section 14. Eminent Domain

Exercise of the power and right of eminent domain shall never be so construed or abridged as to prevent the taking by the legislature of property and franchises of incorporated companies and subjecting them to public use the same as property of individuals.

Section 15. Aid to Railroads and Telegraph Lines Prohibited

Neither the state, nor any county, township, school district or municipality shall loan or give its credit or make donations to or in aid of any railroad or telegraph line; provided, that this section shall not apply to obligations of any county, city, township or school district, contracted prior to the adoption of this constitution.

Section 16. Acceptance of Constitution by Existing Railroad, Transportation and Telegraph Companies

No railroad or other transportation company or telegraph company in existence upon the adoption of this constitution shall derive the benefit of any future legislation without first filing in the office of the secretary of state an acceptance of the provisions of this constitution.

Section 17. Rights of Telegraph Companies

Any association, corporation or lessee of the franchises thereof organized for the purpose shall have the right to construct and maintain lines of telegraph within this state, and to connect the same with other lines.

Section 18. Foreign Railroad or Telegraph Company Must Have Agent for Service of Process

No foreign railroad or telegraph line shall do any business within this state without having an agent or agents within each county through which such railroad or telegraph line shall be constructed upon whom process may be served.

Section 19. Location of Depots

No railroad company shall construct or operate a railroad within four (4) miles of any existing town or city without providing a suitable depot or stopping place at the nearest practicable point for the convenience of said town or city, and stopping all trains doing local business at said stopping place. No railroad company shall deviate from the most direct practicable line in constructing a railroad for the purpose of avoiding the provisions of this section.

ARTICLE 11. BOUNDARIES

Section 1. State Boundaries

The boundaries of the State of Wyoming shall be as follows: Commencing at the intersection of the twenty-seventh meridian of longitude west from Washington with the forty-fifth degree of north latitude, and running thence west to the thirty-fourth meridian of west longitude, thence south to the forty-first degree of north latitude, thence east to the twenty-seventh meridian of west longitude, and thence north to the place of beginning.

ARTICLE 12. COUNTY ORGANIZATION

Section 1. Existing Counties Remain Such

The several counties in the Territory of Wyoming as they shall exist at the time of the admission of said territory as a state, are hereby declared to be counties of the State of Wyoming.

Section 2. Organization of New Counties

The legislature shall provide by general law for organizing new counties, locating the county seats thereof temporarily and changing county lines. But no new county shall be formed unless it shall contain within the limits thereof property of the valuation of two million dollars, as shown by last preceding tax returns, and not then unless the remaining portion of the old county or counties shall each contain property of at least three million dollars of assessable valuation; and no new county shall be organized nor shall any organized county be so reduced as to contain a population of less than one thousand five hundred bona fide inhabitants, and in case any portion of an organized county or counties is stricken off to form a new county, the new county shall assume and be holden for an equitable proportion of the indebtedness of the county or counties so reduced. No county shall be divided unless a majority of the qualified electors of the territory proposed to be cut off voting on the proposition shall vote in favor of the division.

Section 3. Changing County Seats

The legislature shall provide by general law for changing county seats in organized counties, but it shall have no power to remove the county seat of any organized county.

Section 4. Township Organization

The legislature shall provide by general law for a system of township organization and government, which may be adopted by any county whenever a majority of the citizens thereof voting at a general election shall so determine.

Section 5. County Officers

The legislature shall provide by law for the election of such county officers as may be necessary.

ARTICLE 13. MUNICIPAL CORPORATIONS

Section 1. Incorporation; Alteration of Boundaries; Merger; Consolidation; Dissolution; Determination of Local Affairs; Classification; Referendum; Liberal Construction

(a) The legislature shall provide by general law, applicable to all cities and towns,

(i) For the incorporation of cities,

(ii) For the methods by which city and town boundaries may be altered, and

(iii) For the procedures by which cities and towns may be merged, consolidated or dissolved; provided that existing laws on such subjects and laws pertaining to civil service, retirement, collective bargaining, the levying of taxes, excises, fees, or any other charges, whether or not applicable to all cities and towns on the effective date of this amendment, shall remain in effect until superseded by general law and such existing laws shall not be subject to charter ordinance.

(b) All cities and towns are hereby empowered to determine their local affairs and government as established by ordinance passed by the governing body, subject to referendum when prescribed by the legislature, and further subject only to statutes uniformly applicable to all cities and towns, and to statutes prescribing limits of indebtedness. The levying of taxes, excises, fees, or any other charges shall be prescribed by the legislature. The legislature may not establish more than four

(4) classes of cities and towns. Each city and town shall be governed by all other statutes, except as it may exempt itself by charter ordinance as hereinafter provided.

(c) Each city or town may elect that the whole or any part of any statute, other than statutes uniformly applicable to all cities and towns and statutes prescribing limits of indebtedness, may not apply to such city or town. This exemption shall be by charter ordinance passed by a two-thirds (2/3) vote of all members elected to the governing body of the city or town. Each such charter ordinance shall be titled and may provide that the whole or any part of any statute, which would otherwise apply to such city or town as specifically designated in the ordinance shall not apply to such city or town. Such ordinance may provide other provisions on the same subject. Every charter ordinance shall be published once each week for two consecutive weeks in the official city or town newspaper, if any, otherwise in a newspaper of general circulation in the city or town. No charter ordinance shall take effect until the sixtieth (60th) day after its final publication. If prior thereto, a petition, signed by a number of qualified electors of the city or town, equaling at least ten per cent (10%) of the number of votes cast at the last general municipal election, shall be filed in the office of the clerk of such city or town, demanding that such ordinance be submitted to referendum, then the ordinance shall not take effect unless approved by a majority of the electors voting thereon. Such referendum election shall be called within thirty (30) days and held within ninety (90) days after the petition is filed. An ordinance establishing procedures, and fixing the date of such election shall be passed by the governing body and published once each week for three (3) consecutive weeks in the official city or town newspaper, if any, otherwise in a newspaper of general circulation in the city or town. The question on the ballot shall be: "Shall Charter Ordinance No. .... Entitled (stating the title of the ordinance) take effect?". The governing body may submit, without a petition, any charter ordinance to referendum election under the procedures as previously set out. The charter ordinance shall take effect if approved by a majority of the electors voting thereon. An approved charter ordinance, after becoming effective, shall be recorded by the clerk in a book maintained for that purpose with a certificate of the procedures of adoption. A certified copy of the ordinance shall be filed with the secretary of state, who shall keep an index of such ordinances. Each charter ordinance enacted shall prevail over any prior act of the governing body of the city or town, and may be repealed or amended only by subsequent charter ordinance, or by enactments of the legislature applicable to all cities and towns.

(d) The powers and authority granted to cities and towns, pursuant to this section, shall be liberally construed for the purpose of giving the largest measure of self-government to cities and towns.

Section 2. Consent of Electors Necessary

No municipal corporation shall be organized without the consent of the majority of the electors residing within the district proposed to be so incorporated, such consent to be ascertained in the manner and under such regulations as may be prescribed by law.

Section 3. Restriction on Powers to Levy Taxes and Contract Debts

The legislature shall restrict the powers of such corporations to levy taxes and assessments, to borrow money and contract debts so as to prevent the abuse of such power, and no tax or assessment shall be levied or collected or debts contracted by municipal corporations except in pursuance of law for public purposes specified by law.

Section 4. Franchises

No street passenger railway, telegraph, telephone or electric light line shall be constructed within the limits of any municipal organization without the consent of its local authorities.

Section 5. Acquisition of Water Rights

Municipal corporations shall have the same right as individuals to acquire rights by prior appropriation and otherwise to the use of water for domestic and municipal purposes, and the legislature shall provide by law for the exercise upon the part of incorporated cities, towns and villages of the right of eminent domain for the purpose of acquiring from prior appropriators upon the payment of just compensation, such water as may be necessary for the well being thereof and for domestic uses.

ARTICLE 14. PUBLIC OFFICERS

Section 1. Stated Salaries to be Paid

All state, city, county, town and school officers, (excepting justices of the peace and constables in precincts having less than fifteen hundred population, and excepting court commissioners, boards of arbitration and notaries public) shall be paid fixed and definite salaries. The legislature shall, from time to time, fix the amount of such salaries as are not already fixed by this constitution, which shall in all cases be in proportion to the value of the services rendered and the duty performed.

Section 2. Fees

The legislature shall provide by law the fees which may be demanded by justices of the peace and constables in precincts having less than fifteen hundred population, and of court commissioners, boards of arbitration and notaries public, which fees the said officers shall accept as their full compensation. But all other state, county, city, town and school officers shall be required by law to keep a true and correct account of all fees collected by them, and to pay the same into the proper treasury when collected, and the officer whose duty it is to collect such fees shall be held responsible, under his bond, for neglect to collect the same.

Section 3. Legislature to Designate County Offices and Fix Salaries of County Officers

The legislature shall by law designate county offices and shall, from time to time, fix the salaries of county officers, which shall in all cases be in proportion to the value of the services rendered and the duties performed.

Section 4. Deputies

The legislature shall provide by general law for such deputies as the public necessities may require, and shall fix their compensation.

Section 5. Who are County Officers Referred to by Section 3

Any county officers performing the duties usually performed by the officers named in this article shall be considered as referred to by section 3 of this article, regardless of the title by which their offices may hereafter be designated.

Section 6. Consolidation of Offices

Whenever practicable the legislature may, and whenever the same can be done without detriment to the public service, shall consolidate offices in state, county and municipalities respectively, and whenever so consolidated, the duties of such additional office shall be performed under an ex officio title.

ARTICLE 15. TAXATION AND REVENUE

Section 1. Assessment of Lands and Improvements Thereon

All lands and improvements thereon shall be listed for assessment, valued for taxation and assessed separately.

Section 2. Assessment of Coal Lands

All coal lands in the state from which coal is not being mined shall be listed for assessment, valued for taxation and assessed according to value.

Section 3. Taxation of Mines and Mining Claims

All mines and mining claims from which gold, silver and other precious metals, soda, saline, coal, mineral oil or other valuable deposit, is or may be produced shall be taxed in addition to the surface improvements, and in lieu of taxes on the lands, on the gross product thereof, as may be prescribed by law; provided, that the product of all mines shall be taxed in proportion to the value thereof.

Section 4. State Levy Limited

For state revenue, there shall be levied annually a tax not to exceed four mills on the dollar of the assessed valuation of the property in the state except for the support of state educational and charitable institutions, the payment of the state debt and the interest thereon.

Section 5. County Levies Limited

For county revenue, there shall be levied annually a tax not to exceed twelve mills on the dollar for all purposes including general school tax, exclusive of state revenue, except for the payment of its public debt and the interest thereon.

Section 6. City Levies Limited

No incorporated city or town shall levy a tax to exceed eight mills on the dollar in any one year, except for the payment of its public debt and the interest thereon.

Section 7. Depositories for Public Moneys

All money belonging to the state or to any county, city, town, village or other subdivision therein, except as herein otherwise provided, shall, whenever practicable, be deposited in a national bank or banks or in a bank or banks incorporated under the laws of this state; provided, that the bank or banks in which such money is deposited shall furnish security to be approved as provided by law; and provided further, that such bank or banks shall pay the same rate of interest on any money so deposited therein on time certificates of deposit by the legal custodian or custodians of any such public moneys as such bank or banks pay on time certificates of deposit of private depositors, and the custodian or custodians of any such public moneys shall be authorized to deposit same under time certificates of deposit as may be provided by law. Such interest shall accrue to the fund from which it is derived.

Section 8. Profit Making From Public Funds Prohibited

The making of profit, directly or indirectly, out of state, county, city, town or school district money or other public fund, or using the same for any purpose not authorized by law, by any public officer, shall be deemed a felony, and shall be punished as provided by law.

Section 9. Legislature to Provide for State Board of Equalization

The legislature shall provide by law for a state board of equalization.

Section 10. Duties of State Board of Equalization

The duties of the state board shall be to equalize the valuation on all property in the several counties and such other duties as may be prescribed by law.

Section 11. Uniformity of Assessment Required

(a) All property, except as in this constitution otherwise provided, shall be uniformly valued at its full value as defined by the legislature, in three (3) classes as follows:

(i) Gross production of minerals and mine products in lieu of taxes on the land where produced;

(ii) Property used for industrial purposes as defined by the legislature; and

(iii) All other property, real and personal.

(b) The legislature shall prescribe the percentage of value which shall be assessed within each designated class. All taxable property shall be valued at its full value as defined by the legislature except agricultural and grazing lands which shall be valued according to the capability of the land to produce agricultural products under normal conditions. The percentage of value prescribed for industrial property shall not be more than forty percent (40%) higher nor more than four (4) percentage points more than the percentage prescribed for property other than minerals.

(c) The legislature shall not create new classes or subclasses or authorize any property to be assessed at a rate other than the rates set for authorized classes.

(d) All taxation shall be equal and uniform within each class of property. The legislature shall prescribe such regulations as shall secure a just valuation for taxation of all property, real and personal.

Section 12. Exemptions From Taxation

The property of the United States, the state, counties, cities, towns, school districts and municipal corporations, when used primarily for a governmental purpose, and public libraries, lots with the buildings thereon used exclusively for religious worship, church parsonages, church schools and public cemeteries, shall be exempt from taxation, and such other property as the legislature may by general law provide.

Section 13. Tax Must be Authorized by Law; Law to State Object

No tax shall be levied, except in pursuance of law, and every law imposing a tax shall state distinctly the object of the same, to which only it shall be applied.

Section 14. Surrender of Taxing Power Prohibited

The power of taxation shall never be surrendered or suspended by any grant or contract to which the state or any county or other municipal corporation shall be a party.

Section 15. State Tax for Support of Public Schools

For the support of the public schools in the state there may be levied each year a state tax not exceeding twelve mills on the dollar of the assessed valuation of the property in the state.

Section 16. Disposition of Fees, Excises and License Taxes on Vehicles and Gasoline

No moneys derived from fees, excises, or license taxes levied by the state and exclusive of registration fees and licenses or excise taxes imposed by a county or municipality, relating to registration, operation or use of vehicles on public highways, streets or alleys, or to fuels used for propelling such vehicles, shall be expended for other than cost of administering such laws, statutory refunds and adjustments allowed therein, payment of highway obligations, costs for construction, reconstruction, maintenance and repair of public highways, county roads, bridges, and streets, alleys and bridges in cities and towns, and expense of enforcing state traffic laws.

Section 17. County Levy for Support and Maintenance of Public Schools

There shall be levied each year in each county of the state a tax of not to exceed six (6) mills on the dollar of the assessed valuation of the property in each county for the support and maintenance of the public schools. This tax shall be collected by the county treasurer and disbursed among the school districts within the county as the legislature shall provide. The legislature may authorize boards of trustees of school districts to levy a special tax on the property of the district. The legislature may also provide for the distribution among one (1) or more school districts of any revenue from the special school district property tax in excess of a state average yield, which shall be calculated each year, per average daily membership.

Section 18. Full Tax Credit Allowed Against any Liability Arising From a Tax on Income

No tax shall be imposed upon income without allowing full credit against such tax liability for all sales, use, and ad valorem taxes paid in the taxable year by the same taxpayer to any taxing authority in Wyoming.

Section 19. Mineral Excise Tax; Distribution

The Legislature shall provide by law for an excise tax on the privilege of severing or extracting minerals, of one and one-half percent (1 1/2%) on the value of the gross product extracted. The minerals subject to such excise tax shall be coal, petroleum, natural gas, oil shale, and such other minerals as may be designated by the Legislature. Such tax shall be in addition to any other excise, severance or ad valorem tax. The proceeds from such tax shall be deposited in the Permanent Wyoming Mineral Trust Fund. The fund, including all monies deposited in the fund from whatever source, shall remain inviolate. The monies in the fund shall be invested as prescribed by the Legislature and all income from fund investments shall be deposited by the State Treasurer in the general fund on an annual basis. The Legislature may also specify by law, conditions and terms under which monies in the fund may be loaned to political subdivisions of the state.

Section 20. Higher Education Trust Funds; Investments; Earnings

The legislature may from time to time place monies into endowment funds for higher education scholarships and for improving the quality of higher education, which funds shall remain inviolate. The earnings of the funds shall be used for the purposes specified in this section, but the legislature may from time to time by law regulate the manner in which the earnings are expended. The legislature may also provide for use of the earnings to protect the funds from inflation and to even fluctuations in earnings over time. The funds may be invested in the same manner as other permanent funds of the state.

ARTICLE 16. PUBLIC INDEBTEDNESS

Section 1. Limitation on State Debt

The State of Wyoming shall not, in any manner, create any indebtedness exceeding one per centum on the assessed value of the taxable property in the state, as shown by the last general assessment for taxation, preceding; except to suppress insurrection or to provide for the public defense.

Section 2. Creation of State Debt in Excess of Taxes for Current Year

No debt in excess of the taxes for the current year, shall in any manner be created in the State of Wyoming, unless the proposition to create such debt shall have been submitted to a vote of the people and by them approved; except to suppress insurrection or to provide for the public defense.

Section 3. Limitation on County Debt

No county in the State of Wyoming shall in any manner create any indebtedness, exceeding two per centum on the assessed value of taxable property in such county, as shown by the last general assessment, preceding; provided, however, that any county, city, town, village or other subdivision thereof in the State of Wyoming, may bond its public debt existing at the time of the adoption of this constitution, in any sum not exceeding four per centum on the assessed value of the taxable property in such county, city, town, village or other subdivision, as shown by the last general assessment for taxation.

Section 4. Creation of County or Municipal Debt in Excess of Taxes for Current Year

No debt in excess of the taxes for the current year shall, in any manner, be created by any county or subdivision thereof, or any city, town or village, or any subdivision thereof in the State of

Wyoming, unless the proposition to create such debt shall have been submitted to a vote of the people thereof and by them approved.

Section 5. Limitation on Municipal, County or School District Debt

No city or town shall in any manner create any indebtedness exceeding four per cent (4%) of the assessed value of the taxable property therein, except that an additional indebtedness of four per cent (4%) of the assessed value of the taxable property therein may be created for sewage disposal systems. Indebtedness created for supplying water to cities or towns is excepted from the limitation herein.

No county shall in any manner create any indebtedness exceeding two per cent (2%) of the taxable property therein. No school district shall in any manner create any indebtedness exceeding ten per cent (10%) on the assessed value of the taxable property therein for the purpose of acquiring land, erection, enlarging and equipping of school buildings. All limitations herein shall refer to the last preceding general assessment.

Section 6. Loan of Credit; Donations Prohibited; Works of Internal Improvement

Neither the state nor any county, city, township, town, school district, or any other political subdivision, shall loan or give its credit or make donations to or in aid of any individual, association or corporation, except for necessary support of the poor, nor subscribe to or become the owner of the capital stock of any association or corporation, except that funds of public employee retirement systems and the permanent funds of the state of Wyoming may be invested in such stock under conditions the legislature prescribes. The state shall not engage in any work of internal improvement unless authorized by a two-thirds (2/3) vote of the people.

Section 7. Payments of Public Money

No money shall be paid out of the state treasury except upon appropriation by law and on warrant drawn by the proper officer, and no bills, claims, accounts or demands against the state, or any county or political subdivision, shall be audited, allowed or paid until a full itemized statement in writing, certified to under penalty of perjury, shall be filed with the officer or officers whose duty it may be to audit the same.

Section 8. Endorsements Required on Bonds and Other Evidences of Indebtedness

No bond or evidence of indebtedness of the state shall be valid unless the same shall have endorsed thereon a certificate signed by the auditor and secretary of state that the bond or evidence of debt is issued pursuant to law and is within the debt limit. No bond or evidence of debt of any county, or bond of any township or other political subdivision, shall be valid unless the same [shall] have endorsed thereon a certificate signed by the county auditor or other officer authorized by law to sign such certificate, stating that said bond or evidence of debt is issued pursuant to law and is within the debt limit.

Section 9. Construction and Improvement of Public Roads and Highways

The provision of section 6 of article 16 of this constitution prohibiting the state from engaging in any work of internal improvement unless authorized by a two-thirds vote of the people shall not apply to or affect the construction or improvement of public roads and highways; but the legislature shall have power to provide for the construction and improvement of public roads and highways in whole or in part by the state, either directly or by extending aid to counties; and, notwithstanding said inhibition as to works of internal improvement, whenever grants of land or other property shall have been made to the state, especially dedicated by the grant to particular works of internal improvement, the state may carry on such particular works and shall devote thereto the avails of such grants, and may pledge or appropriate the revenues derived from such works in the aid of their completion.

Section 10. Construction and Improvement of Works for Conservation and Utilization of Water

The provisions of section 6 of article 16 of this constitution prohibiting the state from engaging in any work of internal improvements, unless authorized by a two-thirds vote of the people, shall not apply to or affect the construction or improvement of any works designed, constructed or operated for the purposes of conservation or utilization of water, but the legislature shall have the power to provide for the construction or improvement in whole or in part, of any works designed, constructed or operated for the purposes of conservation or utilization of water, either directly or by extending aid to legal subdivisions of the State of Wyoming, duly organized irrigation, drainage, soil conservation, and public irrigation and power districts, and any public corporation legally organized for the purposes of the conservation, distribution or utilization of water or soil; and notwithstanding said inhibition as to works of internal improvement, whenever grants of land or other property shall be made to the state, especially dedicated by the grant to particular works of internal improvement, the state may carry on such particular works of internal improvement and shall devote thereto the avails of such grants, and may likewise pledge or appropriate the revenues derived from such works in aid of their completion.

Section 11. Construction, Maintenance and Improvement of Public Airports, Aircraft Landing Strips and Related Facilities

The provisions of section 6 of article XVI of this constitution prohibiting the state from engaging in any work of internal improvement unless authorized by a two-thirds vote of the people, shall not apply to or affect the construction, maintenance or improvement of public airports, aircraft landing strips and related facilities but the legislature shall have power to provide for the construction, maintenance and improvement of public airports, aircraft landing strips and related facilities, in whole or in part by the state, either directly or by extending aid to its political subdivisions and, notwithstanding said inhibition as to works of internal improvement, whenever grants of land or other property shall have been made to the state, especially dedicated by the grant to particular works of internal improvement, the state may carry on such particular works and shall devote thereto the avails of such grants, and may pledge or appropriate the revenues derived from such works in the aid of their completion and maintenance.

Section 12. Economic Development Loan Fund

(a) Notwithstanding Article 3, Section 36 and Article 16, Sections 1, 2 and 6 of this Constitution, the legislature, by a two-thirds (2/3) vote of all the members of each of the two (2) houses voting separately, may appropriate monies in an amount not exceeding one percent (1%) times the assessed value of the taxable property in the state as shown by the last preceding general assessment for taxation, to provide a revolving investment fund to be used to promote and aid the economic development of the state.

(b) The investment fund created by this section shall be used to provide fully-funded loan guarantees or loans to proposed or existing enterprises which will employ people within the state, provide services within the state, use resources within the state or otherwise add economic value to goods, services or resources within the state.

(c) Monies within the revolving investment fund shall be loaned or used to guarantee loans under such terms and conditions as the legislature may by law direct.

(d) The cumulative total of monies appropriated to provide a revolving investment fund shall never exceed one percent (1%) on the assessed value of the taxable property in the state as shown by the last preceding general assessment for taxation. (e) Notwithstanding the limitation of subsection (d) of this section, earnings on the revolving investment fund shall be added to the revolving investment fund and shall be invested as provided in this section.

Section 13. Industrial and Economic Development; Powers of Counties and Municipalities

Notwithstanding any other provision in this constitution, the legislature may authorize counties or incorporated municipalities, to appropriate from local sources of revenue such funds as may be deemed necessary for an economic or industrial development project or program, public or private, subject to approval by a vote of the majority of the registered voters of the county or municipality voting upon the question. For purposes of this section, "funds from local sources of revenue" means funds raised from general taxes levied by the county or municipality and shall not include any funds received by the county or municipality which are derived from state or federal sources.

ARTICLE 17. STATE MILITIA

Section 1. Of Whom Militia Constituted

The militia of the state shall consist of all able-bodied qualified residents of the state, and those nonresidents who are accepted into service, between the ages of seventeen (17) and seventy (70) years; except those exempted by the law of the United States or of the state. But all residents having scruples of conscience averse to bearing arms shall be excused therefrom upon conditions as shall be prescribed by law.

Section 2. Legislature to Provide for Enrollment, Equipment and Discipline

The legislature shall provide by law for the enrollment, equipment and discipline of the militia to conform as nearly as practicable to the regulations for the government of the armies of the United States.

Section 3. How Officers Commissioned

All militia officers shall be commissioned by the governor, the manner of their selection to be provided by law, and may hold their commission for such period of time as the legislature may provide.

Section 4. Flags

No military organization under the laws of the state shall carry any banner or flag representing any sect or society or the flag of any nationality but that of the United States.

Section 5. Governor to be Commander-in-Chief; Powers

The governor shall be commander-in-chief of all the military forces of the state, and shall have power to call out the militia to preserve the public peace, to execute the laws of the state, to suppress insurrection or repel invasion.

ARTICLE 18. PUBLIC LANDS AND DONATIONS

Section 1. Acceptance of Lands From United States; Sale of Such Lands

The State of Wyoming hereby agrees to accept the grants of lands heretofore made, or that may hereafter be made by the United States to the state, for educational purposes, for public buildings and institutions and for other objects, and donations of money with the conditions and limitations that may be imposed by the act or acts of congress, making such grants or donations. Such lands shall be disposed of only at public auction to the highest responsible bidder, after having been duly appraised by the land commissioners, at not less than three-fourths the appraised value thereof, and for not less than $10 per acre; provided, that in the case of actual and bona fide settlement and improvement thereon at the time of the adoption of this constitution, such actual settler shall have the preference right to purchase the land whereon he may have settled, not exceeding 160 acres at a sum not less than the appraised value thereof, and in making such appraisement the value of improvements shall not be taken into consideration. If, at any time hereafter, the United States shall grant any arid lands in the state to the state, on the condition that the state reclaim and dispose of them to actual settlers, the legislature shall be authorized to accept such arid lands on such conditions, or other conditions, if the same are practicable and reasonable.

Section 2. Application of Proceeds of Sale or Rental

The proceeds from the sale and rental of all lands and other property donated, granted or received, or that may hereafter be donated, granted or received, from the United States or any other source, shall be inviolably appropriated and applied to the specific purposes specified in the original grant or gifts.

Section 3. Board of Land Commissioners

The governor, secretary of state, state treasurer, state auditor and superintendent of public instruction shall constitute a board of land commissioners, which under direction of the legislature as limited by this constitution, shall have direction, control, leasing and disposal of lands of the state granted, or which may be hereafter granted for the support and benefit of public schools, subject to the further limitations that the sale of all lands shall be at public auction, after such delay (not less than the time fixed by congress) in portions at proper intervals of time, and at such minimum prices (not less than the minimum fixed by congress) as to realize the largest possible proceeds. And said board, subject to the limitations of this constitution and under such regulations as may be provided by law shall have the direction, control, disposition and care of all lands that have been heretofore or may hereafter be granted to the state.

Section 4. Legislature to Provide for Disposition of Lands

The legislature shall enact the necessary laws for the sale, disposal, leasing or care of all lands that have been or may hereafter be granted to the state, and shall, at the earliest practicable period, provide by law for the location and selection of all lands that have been or may hereafter be granted by congress to the state, and shall pass laws for the suitable keeping, transfer and disbursement of the land grant funds, and shall require of all officers charged with the same or the safekeeping thereof to give ample bonds for all moneys and funds received by them.

Section 5. Special Privileges Prohibited

Except a preference right to buy as in this constitution otherwise provided, no law shall ever be passed by the legislature granting any privileges to persons who may have settled upon any of the school lands granted to the state subsequent to the survey thereof by the general government, by which the amount to be derived by the sale or other disposition of such lands, shall be diminished directly or indirectly.

Section 6. Disposition of Unexpended Income of Perpetual School Fund

If any portion of the interest or income of the perpetual school fund be not expended during any year, said portion shall be added to and become a part of the said school fund.

ARTICLE 19. MISCELLANEOUS

Livestock

Section 1. Legislature to Provide for Protection of Livestock and Stock Owners

The legislature shall pass all necessary laws to provide for the protection of livestock against the introduction or spread of pleura-pneumonia, glanders, splenetic or Texas fever, and other infectious or contagious diseases. The legislature shall also establish a system of quarantine, or inspection, and such other regulations as may be necessary for the protection of stock owners, and most conducive to the stock interests within the state.

Labor

Section 2. Day's Work

Eight (8) hours actual work shall constitute a lawful day's work in all mines, and on all state and municipal works.

Labor on Public Works

Section 3. Who shall not be employed on public works. No person not a citizen of the United States or who has not declared his intention to become such, shall be employed upon or in connection with any state, county or municipal works or employment.

Section 4. Legislature to Provide for Enforcement of Section 3

The legislature shall, by appropriate legislation, see that the provisions of the foregoing section are enforced.

Boards of Arbitration

Section 5. Legislature to Establish Courts of Arbitration; Duties

Repealed

Police Powers

Section 6. Importing Armed Bodies to Suppress Violence Prohibited; Exception

No armed police force, or detective agency, or armed body, or unarmed body of men, shall ever be brought into this state, for the suppression of domestic violence, except upon the application of the legislature, or executive, when the legislature cannot be convened.

Labor Contracts

Section 7. Contract Exempting Employer from Liability for Personal Injuries Prohibited

It shall be unlawful for any person, company or corporation, to require of its servants or employes as a condition of their employment, or otherwise, any contract or agreement whereby such person, company or corporation shall be released or discharged from liability or responsibility, on account of personal injuries received by such servants or employes, while in the service of such person, company or corporation, by reason of the negligence of such person, company or corporation, or the agents or employes thereof, and such contracts shall be absolutely null and void.

Arbitration

Section 8. Legislature to Provide for Voluntary Submission of Differences to Arbitrators

The legislature may provide by law for the voluntary submission of differences to arbitrators for determination and said arbitrators shall have such powers and duties as may be prescribed by law; but they shall have no power to render judgment to be obligatory on parties; unless they voluntarily submit their matters of difference and agree to abide the judgment of such arbitrators.

Homesteads

Section 9. Exemption of Homestead

A homestead as provided by law shall be exempt from forced sale under any process of law, and shall not be alienated without the joint consent of husband and wife, when that relation exists; but no property shall be exempt from sale for taxes, or for the payment of obligations contracted for the purchase of said premises, or for the erection of improvements thereon.

Intoxicating Liquors

Section 10. Intoxicating Liquors

On and after the first day of March, 1935, the manufacture, sale and keeping for sale of malt, vinous or spirituous liquors, wine, ale, porter, beer or any intoxicating drink, mixture or preparation of like nature may be permitted in the State of Wyoming under such regulation as the legislature may prescribe.

Section 11. Use of Monies in Public Employee Retirement Funds Restricted

All monies from any source paid into any public employee retirement system created by the laws of this state shall be used only for the benefit of the members, retirees and beneficiaries of that system, including the payment of system administrative costs.

ARTICLE 20. AMENDMENTS

Section 1. How Amendments Proposed by Legislature and Submitted to People

Any amendment or amendments to this constitution may be proposed in either branch of the legislature, and, if the same shall be agreed to by two-thirds of all the members of each of the two houses, voting separately, such proposed amendment or amendments shall, with the yeas and nays thereon, be entered on their journals, and it shall be the duty of the legislature to submit such amendment or amendments to the electors of the state at the next general election, and cause the same to be published without delay for at least twelve (12) consecutive weeks, prior to said election, in at least one newspaper of general circulation, published in each county, and if a majority of the electors shall ratify the same, such amendment or amendments shall become a part of this constitution.

Section 2. How Two or More Amendments Voted On

If two or more amendments are proposed, they shall be submitted in such manner that the electors shall vote for or against each of them separately.

Section 3. Constitutional Convention

Whenever two-thirds of the members elected to each branch of the legislature shall deem it necessary to call a convention to revise or amend this constitution, they shall recommend to the electors to vote at the next general election for or against a convention, and if a majority of all the electors voting at such election shall have voted for a convention, the legislature shall at the next session provide by law for calling the same; and such convention shall consist of a number of members, not less than double that of the most numerous branch of the legislature.

Section 4. Constitution Adopted by Convention to be Submitted to People

Any constitution adopted by such convention shall have no validity until it has been submitted to and adopted by the people.

ARTICLE 21. SCHEDULE

Section 1. Acquired Rights Continue

That no inconvenience may arise from a change of the territorial government to a permanent state government, it is declared that all writs, actions, prosecutions, claims, liabilities and obligations against the Territory of Wyoming, of whatever nature, and rights of individuals, and of bodies corporate, shall continue as if no change had taken place in this government, and all process which may, before the organization of the judicial department under this constitution, be issued under the authority of the Territory of Wyoming, shall be as valid as if issued in the name of the state.

Section 2. Territorial Property Vested in State

All property, real and personal, and all moneys, credits, claims and choses in action, belonging to the Territory of Wyoming, at the time of the adoption of this constitution, shall be vested in and become the property of the State of Wyoming.

Section 3. Territorial Laws Become State Laws

All laws now in force in the Territory of Wyoming, which are not repugnant to this constitution, shall remain in force until they expire by their own limitation, or be altered or repealed by the legislature.

Section 4. Accrued Fines go to State

All fines, penalties, forfeitures and escheats, accruing to the Territory of Wyoming, shall accrue to the use of the state.

Section 5. State to Sue on Bonds and Prosecute Crimes

All recognizances, bonds, obligations or other undertakings heretofore taken, or which may be taken before the organization of the judicial department under this constitution shall remain valid, and shall pass over to and may be prosecuted in the name of the state, and all bonds, obligations or other undertakings executed to this territory, or to any officer in his official capacity, shall pass over to the proper state authority and to their successors in office, for the uses therein respectively expressed, and may be sued for and recovered accordingly. All criminal prosecutions and penal actions which have arisen or which may arise before the organization of the judicial department under this constitution, and which shall then be pending, may be prosecuted to judgment and execution in the name of the state.

Section 6. Territorial Officers to Hold Over

All officers, civil and military, holding their offices and appointments in this territory, under the authority of the United States or under the authority of this territory, shall continue to hold and exercise their respective offices and appointments until suspended under this constitution.

Section 7. Submission of Constitution

This constitution shall be submitted for adoption or rejection to a vote of the qualified electors of this territory, at an election to be held on the first Tuesday in November, A. D. 1889. Said election, as nearly as may be, shall be conducted in all respects in the same manner as provided by the laws of the territory for general elections, and the returns thereof shall be made to the secretary of said territory, who with the governor and chief justice thereof, or any two of them, shall canvass the same, and if a majority of the legal votes cast shall be for the constitution the governor shall certify the result to the president of the United States, together with a statement of the votes cast thereon and a copy of said constitution, articles, propositions and ordinances. At the said election the ballots shall be in the following form: "For the constitution—Yes. No." And as a heading to each of said ballots, shall be printed on each ballot the following instructions to voters: "All persons who desire to vote for the constitution may erase the word 'No.' All persons who desire to vote against the constitution may erase the word 'Yes.'" Any person may have printed or written on his ballot only the words: "For the Constitution," or "Against the Constitution," and such ballots shall be counted for or against the constitution accordingly.

Section 8. When Constitution Takes Effect

This constitution shall take effect and be in full force immediately upon the admission of the territory as a state.

Section 9. First State Election; Time of Holding; Proclamation

Immediately upon the admission of the territory as a state, the governor of the territory, or in case of his absence or failure to act, the secretary of the territory, or in case of his absence or failure to act, the president of this convention, shall issue a proclamation, which shall be published and a copy thereof mailed to the chairman of the board of county commissioners of each county, calling an election by the people for all state, district and other officers, created and made elective by this constitution, and fixing a day for such election, which shall not be less than forty days after the date of such proclamation nor more than ninety days after the admission of the territory as a state.

Section 10. First State Election; Duty of County Commissioners; Who May Vote; Conduct of Election

The board of commissioners of the several counties shall thereupon order such election for said day, and shall cause notice thereof to be given, in the manner and for the length of time provided by the laws of the territory in cases of general elections for delegate to congress, and county and other officers. Every qualified elector of the territory at the date of said election shall be entitled to vote thereat. Said election shall be conducted in all respects in the same manner as provided by the laws of the territory for general elections, and the returns thereof shall be made to the canvassing board hereinafter provided for.

Section 11. First State Election; Board of Canvassers

The governor, secretary of the territory and president of this convention, or a majority of them, shall constitute a board of canvassers to canvass the vote of such election for member of congress, all state and district officers and members of the legislature. The said board shall assemble at the seat of government of the territory on the thirtieth day after the day of such election (or on the following day if such day fall on Sunday) and proceed to canvass the votes for all state and district officers and members of the legislature, in the manner provided by the laws of the territory for canvassing the vote for delegate to congress, and they shall issue certificates of election to the persons found to be elected to said offices, severally, and shall make and file with the secretary of the territory an abstract certified by them of the number of votes cast for each person, for each of said offices, and of the total number of votes cast in each county.

Section 12. When Officers Shall Qualify; Oaths; Bonds

All officers elected at such election, except members of the legislature, shall, within thirty days after they have been declared elected, take the oath required by this constitution, and give the same bond required by law of the territory to be given in case of like officers of the territory or district, and shall thereupon enter upon the duties of their respective offices; but the legislature may require by law all such officers to give other or further bonds as a condition of their continuance in office.

Section 13. First State Legislature

The governor elect of the state, immediately upon his qualifying and entering upon the duties of his office, shall issue his proclamation convening the legislature of the state at the seat of government, on a day to be named in said proclamation, and which shall not be less than thirty nor more than sixty days after the date of such proclamation. Within ten days after the organization of the legislature, both houses of the legislature, in joint session, shall then there proceed to elect, as provided by law, two senators of the United States for the State of Wyoming. At said election the two persons who shall receive the majority of all the votes cast by said senators and representatives shall be elected as such United States senators, and shall be so declared by the presiding officers of said joint session. The presiding officers of the senate and house shall issue a certificate to each of said senators, certifying his election, which certificates shall also be signed by the governor and attested by the secretary of state.

Section 14. Laws to be Passed

The legislature shall pass all necessary laws to carry into effect the provisions of this constitution.

Section 15. Transfer of Pending Causes, Records and Seal of Courts

Whenever any two of the judges of the supreme court of the state, elected under the provisions of this constitution, shall have qualified in their offices, the causes then pending in the supreme court of the territory, and the papers, records and proceedings of said court, and the seal and other property pertaining thereto, shall pass into the jurisdiction and possession of the supreme court of the state; and until so superseded the supreme court of the territory and the judges thereof shall continue with like powers and jurisdiction, as if this constitution had not been adopted. Whenever the judge of the district court of any district, elected under the provisions of this constitution, shall have qualified in office, the several causes then pending in the district court of the territory, within any county in such district, and the records, papers and proceedings of said district court and the seal and other property pertaining thereto, shall pass into the jurisdiction and possession of the district court of the state for such county; and until the district courts of this territory shall be superseded in the manner aforesaid, the said district courts and the judges thereof shall continue with the same jurisdiction and power to be exercised in the same judicial districts respectively as heretofore constituted under the laws of the territory.

Section 16. Court Seals

Until otherwise provided by law the seals now in use in the supreme and district courts of this territory are hereby declared to be the seals of the supreme and district courts, respectively, of the state.

Section 17. Transfer of Causes and Records From Probate Courts to District Courts

Whenever this constitution shall go into effect, records and papers and proceedings of the probate court in each county, and all causes and matters of administration and other matters pending therein, shall pass into the jurisdiction and possession of the district court of the same county, and the said district court shall proceed to final decree or judgment order or other determination in the said several matters and causes, as the said probate court might have done if this constitution had not been adopted.

Section 18. How Legislature Chosen

Senators and members of the house of representatives shall be chosen by the qualified electors of the several senatorial and representative districts as established in this constitution, until such districts shall be changed by law, and thereafter by the qualified electors of the several districts as the same shall be established by law.

Section 19. Duration of Terms of Territorial County and Precinct Officers

All county and precinct officers who may be in office at the time of the adoption of this constitution, shall hold their respective offices for the full time for which they may have been elected, and until such time as their successors may be elected and qualified, as may be provided by law, and the official bonds of all such officers shall continue in full force and effect as though this constitution had not been adopted.

Section 20. Terms of State Officers First Elected

Members of the legislature and all state officers, district and supreme judges elected at the first election held under this constitution shall hold their respective offices for the full term next ensuing such election, in addition to the period intervening between the date of their qualification and the commencement of such full term.

Section 21. Regular Session of Legislature Following First Session

If the first session of the legislature under this constitution shall be concluded within twelve months of the time designated for a regular session thereof, then the next regular session following said special session shall be omitted.

Section 22. Regular Election Following First Session of Legislature to be Omitted

The first regular election that would otherwise occur following the first session of the legislature, shall be omitted, and all county and precinct officers elected at the first election held under this constitution shall hold their office for the full term thereof, commencing at the expiration of the term of the county and precinct officers then in office, or the date of their qualification.

Section 23. Why Constitution Framed

This convention does hereby declare on behalf of the people of the Territory of Wyoming, that this constitution has been prepared and submitted to the people of the Territory of Wyoming for their adoption or rejection, with no purpose of setting up or organizing a state government until such time as the congress of the United States shall enact a law for the admission of the Territory of Wyoming as a state under its provisions.

ORDINANCES

The following article [sections] shall be irrevocable without the consent of the United States and the people of this state:

Section 24. State Part of United States

The State of Wyoming is an inseparable part of the federal union and the constitution of the United States is the supreme law of the land.

Section 25. Religious Liberty

Perfect toleration of religious sentiment shall be secured, and no inhabitant of this state shall ever be molested in person or property on account of his or her mode of religious worship.

Section 26. Ownership of Certain Lands Disclaimed; Restriction on Taxation of Nonresidents

The people inhabiting this state do agree and declare that they forever disclaim all right and title to the unappropriated public lands lying within the boundaries thereof, and to all lands lying within said limits owned or held by any Indian or Indian tribes, and that until the title thereto shall have been extinguished by the United States, the same shall be and remain subject to the disposition of the United States and that said Indian lands shall remain under the absolute jurisdiction and control of the congress of the United States; that the lands belonging to the citizens of the United States residing without this state shall never be taxed at a higher rate than the lands belonging to residents of this state; that no taxes shall be imposed by this state on lands or property therein, belonging to, or which may hereafter be purchased by the United States, or reserved for its use. But nothing in this article shall preclude this state from taxing as other lands are taxed, any lands owned or held by any Indian who has severed his tribal relations, and has obtained from the United States or from any person, a title thereto, by patent or other grant, save and except such lands as have been or may be granted to any Indian or Indians under any acts of congress containing a provision exempting the lands thus granted from taxation, which last mentioned lands shall be exempt from taxation so long, and to such an extent, as is, or may be provided in the act of congress granting the same.

Section 27. Territorial Liabilities Assumed

All debts and liabilities of the Territory of Wyoming shall be assumed and paid by this state.

Section 28. Legislature to Provide for Public Schools

The legislature shall make laws for the establishment and maintenance of systems of public schools which shall be open to all the children of the state and free from sectarian control.

Done in open convention, at the City of Cheyenne, in the Territory of Wyoming, this 30th day of September in the year of our Lord one thousand eight hundred and eighty-nine.

Attested:

MELVILLE C. BROWN

JOHN K. JEFFREY, President, Secretary

GEO. W. BAXTER	ASBURY B. CONAWAY
H. G. NICKERSON	GEO. W. FOX
A. C. CAMPBELL	HENRY S. ELLIOTT
A. L. SUTHERLAND	FRANK M. FOOTE
J. A. CASEBEER	MORTIMER N. GRANT
W. E. CHAPLIN	CHAS. H. BURRITT
C. D. CLARK	HENRY G. HAY
JONATHAN JONES	CHAS. N. POTTER,
HENRY A. COFFEEN	FREDERICK H. HARVEY
JOHN L. RUSSELL	D. A. PRESTON

MARK HOPKINS
JOHN A. RINER
JOHN W. HOYT
GEO. C. SMITH
WM. C. IRVINE
H. E. TESCHEMACHER
JAMES A. JOHNSTON
C. L. VAGNER
JESSE KNIGHT
THOS. R. REID
ELLIOTT N. MORGAN
ROBT. C. BUTLER

EDWARD J. MORRIS
C. W. BURDICK
JOHN M. MCCANDLISH
DE FOREST RICHARDS
HERMAN F. MENOUGH
MEYER FRANK
CALEB P. ORGAN
M. C. BARROW
LOUIS J. PALMER
RICHARD H. SCOTT
C. W. HOLDEN

www.ingramcontent.com/pod-product-compliance
Lightning Source LLC
Chambersburg PA
CBHW071551220526
45469CB00003B/982